YASUO KUNIYOSHI:
ARTIST AS PHOTOGRAPHER

Catalogue essays by
Franklin Riehlman & Tom Wolf
and Bruce Weber

Published by the
Edith C. Blum Art Institute
Milton and Sally Avery Arts Center
Bard College Center
with the
Norton Gallery and School of Art

INTRODUCTION

Cover and book design by
John O'Mara
Printed at Morgan and Morgan, Inc.,
Dobbs Ferry, New York
Publishers of Photographic Literature

Cover photograph:
Yasuo Kuniyoshi, *Black Man on Beach,*
1938; 7-3/8 × 9-3/8"

This exhibition is funded in part by a grant
from the National Endowment for the Arts.
It was organized by the Edith C. Blum Art
Institute with the cooperation of the
Norton Gallery and School of Art.

The information that is presented in this catalogue focuses on the distinguished career of Yasuo Kuniyoshi. It addresses the specific issue of how this artist, whose unique style is characterized by the willful distortion of appearances, migrated so comfortably into the medium of photography. The camera is mechanically equipped to serve as a neutral recording device; as such, it would appear incompatible with Kuniyoshi's highly expressive aesthetic requirements. Yet through his inventive use of this medium, he was able to manipulate the resulting image so that it ultimately assumed a stylistic consistency with his paintings, drawings and lithographs.

His task was greatly facilitated by the popularization of the newly designed 35mm camera. Because this camera was fast, unobtrusive, mobile and flexible, it expanded the range of photographic options far beyond the parameters imposed by earlier, more cumbersome cameras.

Kuniyoshi was not the only artist to become involved with this new medium for creative expression. His enthusiasm for the 35mm camera was shared by other highly regarded American painters during the era of the 1930s. These include Reginald Marsh, Ben Shahn, Konrad Cramer, Ralston Crawford, and Rockwell Kent. The last section provides examples of their photographic work. Each explored the visual environment from this expanded range of photographic possibilities providing artists with the opportunity to select, without technical limitation, motif, subject, spatial orientation, and formal organization. In general, the tendency to produce images that were static, frontal and premeditated was replaced by the opportunity to work spontaneously, capturing candid and dynamic moments from unexpected vantage points. Photography became capable of responding to the rhythms and tempos of contemporary life.

Linda Weintraub

Konrad Cramer, Yasuo Kuniyoshi With His Camera. *Copy print from an original negative. c. 1937.*

ACKNOWLEDGEMENTS

Sara Kuniyoshi is a petite and gracious woman who has inherited the responsibility of monitoring and managing the life's work of her esteemed late husband, the artist Yasuo Kuniyoshi. It is with sincere appreciation to her that the Edith C. Blum Art Institute and the Norton Gallery and School of Art are privileged to exhibit an important aspect of Kuniyoshi's career that has never before been available to the public. Ms. Kuniyoshi has allowed us to examine, select, and exhibit a collection of photographs that were taken by her husband between 1935 and 1939. These photographs, labeled and dated by the artist, have remained in her possession all of these years. Presenting them in conjunction with examples of Kuniyoshi's work in other media reveals fresh insights into his approach to subject matter and his compositional decision-making process. In addition, they provide new information about the complex relationship between painting and photography during the 1930s. But most important, the images are extraordinary. Kuniyoshi exploited the flexibility of the newly invented 35mm camera. He explored the vastly enlarged range of photographic options that this camera had made available to photographers. In the process, he created photographs that remain fresh and inventive even to today's audience.

Sara Kuniyoshi participated in every phase of this project. She supplied documents, resources, and personal recollections, guiding the curatorial and scholarly efforts of Franklin Riehlman, Bruce Weber and Tom Wolf. Their academic compatibility, along with a determination to uncover and explain every clue to Kuniyoshi's unique sensibility that lay within his body of photographs and still lifes, has produced an impressive amount of new information. The collaboration of these three scholars has produced a document that will make a permanent and significant contribution to the literature on American art and photography.

This exhibition, originally proposed by Tom Wolf and Franklin Riehlman, and developed in conjunction with Bruce Weber, was funded, in part, by the National Endowment for the Arts. Its support has provided both the funding and the credibility that facilitated every phase of the preparation for the exhibition and the catalogue. This contribution was augmented by the tireless efforts of Arnold Davis who, as an alumnus of Bard College and a connoisseur of art, participated in raising additional funding for the project. Gratitude is extended to the Endowment and to Mr. Davis, as well as to Tara Kawa, Anthony Evan Hecht, Jin Kinoshita, Ralph Kahana, and Richard Hamilton for their generous assistance.

Several members of the staffs of both exhibiting institutions deserve special mention for their professional involvement with the exhibition. They include, at Bard College, Donise English, Karla Paschkis, Mike Prudhom, Brian O'Sullivan, and Tina Iraca, who fulfilled their responsibilities regarding the loans, the installations, and the publicity for this exhibition with great skill, assuring the protection of the work and the beauty of its presentation. Gratitude is also extended to Dimitri Papadimitriou for the assistance he has offered through the Bard College Center. At the Norton Gallery and School of Art, Esther Grapes, Research Assistant, collaborated on the compilation of charts tracing Kuniyoshi's development as a still life painter, and Nancy Barrow, Curatorial Assistant, and Pamela Parry, Registrar, both of whom are to be commended for their efforts on behalf of the organization of the exhibition.

The study of Kuniyoshi's photographs received invaluable assistance thanks to the knowledgeable and generous cooperation of David Anderson, Belinda Bacon, Lawrence Campbell and Rosina Florio of the Art Students League, Karl and Lillian Fortess, Rosella Hartman, Anne Helioff Hirschberg, Hal Hisey, Victoria Hoffman, Russell Lee and Steven Miller of the Museum of the City of New York, and Arnold Newman, Andrée Ruellan, Gert Schiff, Gary Snyder, Harry Sternberg, John Taylor, and Dorothy Varian.

CONTENTS

Special appreciation is extended to Howard Green-berg, Steven Shore, Sandra Phillips, and the Daniel Wolf Gallery. All were instrumental in arranging for the exhibition. Furthermore, Doug Morgan guided our efforts, not only designing and printing the catalogue, but sharing with us both his knowledge and his friends who became yet another source of information. Through him we received valuable suggestions from Beaumont Newhall, Karl Kleinen, Rolf Fricke, Helen Wright, Karl Keller, and Barbara Morgan.

Finally, the cooperation of the lenders to this exhibition has made possible an exhibition of extraordinary range and significance. On behalf of the many visitors who will benefit from their willingness to participate in this project, gratitude is extended to:

The Albright-Knox Gallery
The Art Institute of Chicago
The Honolulu Academy of Art
Paul Jenkins
Sara M. Kuniyoshi
The Metropolitan Museum of Art
The Museum of Modern Art
Norton Gallery and School of Art
Photofind Gallery
Private Collection, Florida
Andree Ruellen
The Santa Barbara Museum of Art
The Sheldon Memorial Art Gallery
James Sullivan
The Walker Art Center
The Whitney Museum of American Art

Linda Weintraub, Director
Edith C. Blum Art Institute

Richard A. Madigan, Director
The Norton Gallery and School of Art

1. Yasuo Kuniyoshi, Self Portrait with Camera, *1923, oil on canvas,*
20 × 30". Formerly on loan to the Worcester Art Museum.

Yasuo Kuniyoshi,
Painter/Photographer

by Franklin Riehlman and Tom Wolf

In late December 1941, Yasuo Kuniyoshi, one of the best-known artists in the United States, was required to appear at his local police precinct in New York City. The Japanese had just attacked Pearl Harbor and, although he considered himself an American artist and had lived in the United States thirty-five years, he was still a Japanese citizen. (The Japanese had not been allowed to become American citizens since 1924.[1]) Although he had publicly opposed Japanese military aggression in Manchuria,[2] Kuniyoshi was considered an enemy alien. He was restricted to his studio,[3] the Treasury Department impounded his finances,[4] and the Justice Department informed him he could not leave New York City without its approval.[5] At the police precinct he surrendered his radio, binoculars and 35mm Leica camera.[6]

Today Kuniyoshi's loss of his camera takes on new implications because he was seriously involved with photography in the late 1930s. He took and printed over 400 photographs between 1935 and 1939. Knowledge of these prints adds a new dimension to Kuniyoshi's career, placing him in the company of Charles Sheeler, Ben Shahn, Reginald Marsh, Ralston Crawford, and Konrad Cramer, American painter-photographers of the 1930s.

Kuniyoshi's photographs, and photographic work by painters in general, raise different issues than do pictures taken by professionals. They pose the question of how they connect to his paintings. Some of Kuniyoshi's photographs portray the same subjects that inspired his paintings, drawings, and lithographs, and share stylistic elements with them. He also incorporated a few of his photographs into still-life paintings, where they have a symbolic function essential to the meanings of these works. Some of his photographs are like snapshots, providing information about his life and activities. But Kuniyoshi was a visually sophisticated professional painter and his best photographs stand on their own as independent works. Together they form a group comparable in breadth and originality to the photographs taken by any painter. The photographs Kuniyoshi took and printed express the same sensibility that animates the rest of his production, and are of the same quality.

* * *

Kuniyoshi was 47 years old when he purchased his Leica in 1935. He had emigrated from Japan in 1906 at the age of 17.[7] After four years on the West Coast he moved to New York City and in 1916 he enrolled at the Art Students League where he studied with Kenneth Hayes Miller. He spent the summers of 1918 through 1922 studying at Hamilton Easter Field's Oguniquit (Maine) School of Painting and Sculpture. There, in 1919, he married Katherine Schmidt, whom he had met at the League. She lost her American citizenship upon their marriage. Her parents did not approve of the union and cut the couple off from financial support.[8]

At this point, Kuniyoshi took up photography for the first time. Needing a job that would provide his share of the couple's income and would still allow him enough time and energy to paint, he decided to photograph works of art. In a 1940 article, Kuniyoshi reminisced about his job:

Frequent exhibitions in themselves were not sufficiently remunerative, so I had to turn to something more substantial to keep me going. I don't know why I chose photography as a way to earn a living. I bought a regular studio camera and practised by using my own canvases as models. Photography agreed with me for I learned quickly and in between painting I received commissions from friends and galleries for photographing sculpture and painting. The winters were spent in this fashion and in the summer I devoted my time to painting in Ogunquit.[9]

His friend and fellow painter, Alexander Brook, also remembered Kuniyoshi's activity as a photographer of works of art:

Yas, in order to meet the pressing need for some financial stability, bought a camera—a large cumbersome one—and was soon in demand by artists, museums, and galleries needing photographs of paintings. Going from place to place lugging his camera and other necessary photographic paraphernalia consumed too much of Yas's time and energy.[10]

The Daniel Gallery, where Kuniyoshi, in 1922, had his first one-man show, was one of several art galleries that hired him to document their paintings, sculptures, and objets d'art and the famous collectors, the H.O. Havemeyers, were among the collectors who employed him.[11]

Around 1923, Kuniyoshi made a charming small print, in his early primitive style, to advertise his photographic business (il. 2).[12] It shows a formally dressed man taking a picture in a coastal landscape animated by plants, a whale, and a clipper ship.

In 1924, the artist documented his years as a professional photographer in an important painting, *Self-Portrait with Camera* (il. 1). Kuniyoshi created a stylized self-image, depicting himself in an awkward pose and eccentric garb (the photographer's hood) that anticipate his famous *Self-Portrait as Golf Player* (1927).[13] Critic Henry McBride thought that *Self-Portrait with Camera* was the best painting in Kuniyoshi's show at the Daniel Gallery in 1925, and he interpreted its imagery as did most of the writers at the time: "The artist shows himself at a window equipped for snapping the landscape."[14] But another critic, Forbes Watson, read the painting differently, preferring to see

2. *Yasuo Kuniyoshi,* Photographer on the Beach, *c. 1925, linocut, business card. Collection of Dorothea Greenbaum, Princeton.*

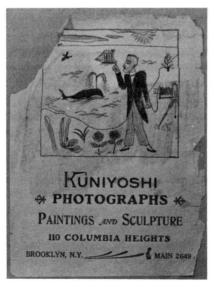

Kuniyoshi in the act of taking a portrait: "We find Mr. Kuniyoshi about to tell the patient to smile, please. He is taking a photograph."[15] This disagreement points to a basic ambiguity in the work—it is unclear what the artist is photographing. Since he was a photographer of works of art, another interpretation is that he shows himself taking a picture of a landscape painting, rather than the landscape itself. The barren tree with its spiky branches appears in many of his early paintings and drawings, and we know he photographed his own works. Kuniyoshi here probes the levels of reality and ambiguity that can be included in a work of visual art. Although his art has rarely been analyzed in these terms, he raises such issues in numerous later works, where they are often linked to photography.

*   *   *

After his 1925 show at the Daniel Gallery, Kuniyoshi took his first trip to Europe, and remained for ten months. Early in 1928 he returned for another ten-month stay. By then he was financially able to give up his job as a photographer of works of art. This second European sojourn proved to be of great importance for the development of his painting. He later recalled,

The trip proved a great stimulus, enlarging my scope and vision. Almost everybody on the other side was painting directly from the object, something I hadn't done all these years. It was rather difficult to change my approach since up to then I had painted almost entirely from my imagination and my memories of the past.[16]

Painting directly from the object enriched both the form and content of his still life paintings, and still life became the area where Kuniyoshi achieved his most original and complex expression (see the following essay by Bruce Weber). Part of this new complexity came from his inclusion of photographs as objects in his still lifes, expanding their range of reference beyond that of more conventional still lifes.

Weather Vane and Other Objects (1933, il. 18) includes a photographic reproduction of Goya's *Portrait of Tadias Arias de Enriquez.*[17] By its inclusion, Kuniyoshi pays homage to Goya. He also acknowledges other aspects of his artistic heritage: the magazine, *Cahiers d'Art*, evokes his appreciation of modern French art, while the galloping horse—an iron weather vane—affirms his affection for American folk art.[18] The sculpture mold placed in the middle of these objects was borrowed from his friend, Paul Fiene.[19] Its presence in the painting seems to be a tribute to the sculptor, and by extension, to the artist colony in Woodstock, New York, where Fiene lived and Kuniyoshi spent his summers.[20]

In the 1934 painting, *Still Life*,[21] Kuniyoshi pays his respect to one of the masters of the School of Paris by placing a fruit bowl and a scarf upon a reproduction of Henri Matisse's *Woman in a Hat*.[22] With *Artificial Flower and Other Things* (il. 22), which he executed as a painting and a lithograph in 1934, Kuniyoshi developed levels of meaning much more intricate than in *Still Life*, and again they center around the reproduction of a work of art. In this case the work is Titian's *Mary Magdalene*,[23] and once more Kuniyoshi makes the medium of the reproduction ambiguous—we cannot tell if it is a photograph, or a print, or some other type of copy. We know that the Goya and the Titian were painted from photographs because the photographs still exist in the Kuniyoshi house in Woodstock.

The question of the medium of the reproduction in *Artificial Flower and Other Things* is only one of the several ambiguities in this painting. The title is typically idiosyncratic, and indicates the key issue of the painting: which is the artificial flower? The flower in the vase would seem to be the artificial one in question, but in paint we cannot tell. Since everything is rendered in paint, everything is artificial. The flowers on the vase are doubly false, painted on the vase before it was depicted by Kuniyoshi, just as leaves are printed on the scarf below the vase. Characteristically, Kuniyoshi's painting also has a personal meaning, a meaning that can be understood thanks to the artist's second wife, Sara Mazo Kuniyoshi. She reports that "artificial flower" was an expression used by Kuniyoshi and Katherine Schmidt. The phrase, which Schmidt applied to women Kuniyoshi found attractive, in effect meant a "passing fancy." The *Mary Magdalene* that crowns the composition is ambivalent in its own right, combining piety and sensuality. Titian scholar David Rosand points out it is "a religious image, overt in the sensuality of its appeal, that at once inspires devotion and sustains delectation."[24]

*   *   *

Kuniyoshi's inclusion of photographically reproduced images in his paintings indicates the pervasiveness of reproductions by the mid-1930s. This phenomenon was linked to a technical development in the field: the introduction of the "miniature" camera. These light, easily portable cameras became widely available in 1924. The

market was dominated by the 35mm Leica, the model Kuniyoshi used. This camera quickly became popular with the public; for the first time it was easy to capture candid moments, often from off or previously inaccessible angles. The 35mm camera gave rise to modern photojournalism, and encouraged the development of illustrated tabloid newspapers and picture magazines which appear in many of Kuniyoshi's still-life and figure paintings.[25]

Painters, like the general public, were quick to recognize the possibilities of the new camera. A number of Kuniyoshi's friends, including Konrad Cramer and Emil Ganso, who, like Kuniyoshi, were expatriot artists working in Woodstock, owned "miniature" cameras by 1935. A photograph from a few years later shows the three artists together with their cameras (il. 3). It is quite possible that Cramer and Ganso encouraged Kuniyoshi to become involved with photography.

3. *Anonymous,* Konrad Cramer, Emil Ganso and Yasuo Kuniyoshi, c. 1938, photograph. Collection of Sara M. Kuniyoshi, New York.

Kuniyoshi had his 35mm camera by 1935. This date is established by Sara Kuniyoshi, who recalls that he refused to take a picture of the Grand Canyon when they were travelling through the Southwest and Mexico on a Guggenheim fellowship in that year. She remembers him saying, "How can I photograph this?—I can buy a post card." It is possible to date many of Kuniyoshi's photographs because he kept most of them in folders, which he labelled with the subject and date of the pictures inside. The first photograph he dated is from 1937, the year he set up a dark room in his Woodstock studio.

* * *

One photograph does exist from the 1935 trip to Mexico (fig. 1). It announces many of the qualities that will be found in Kuniyoshi's photographs of the later 1930s, such as the sensitivity to textures, the cropping of figures at the lower edge, the diagonal movement into space, and the building of a shallow space up the picture plane. The glossy finish is unusual because he eventually favored matte prints. Also unusual is the dissolving of the image at the top; perhaps he was unfamiliar with printing 35mm negatives.

Western Landscape (il. 4), a lithograph from 1935, shares many characteristics with this photograph: the play of diagonals, the shallow space, the juxtaposition of domestic animals with architecture, and the identical motif of the grazing horse. Does this mean that the lithograph was taken from the photograph? Unlikely, and beside the point. Kuniyoshi's sensibility is manifest in his photographs as well as in his better-known works in those media traditionally considered part of the painter's repertoire: painting, drawing, and lithography. The same artist who

4. Yasuo Kuniyoshi, Western Landscape, *1935, lithograph, 11-1/8 × 14-13/16". Collection of Museum of Modern Art. Gift of Grace Borgenicht.*

drew *Western Landscape* on the lithographic stone and critically examined the print when it came out of the press also snapped the Mexican photograph and critically examined the print when it came out of its chemical bath.

Western Landscape and the photograph are independent of each other, yet connected by the artist's vision. But in one case there is a direct correspondence: a Coney Island photograph that Kuniyoshi used as the source for his 1936 lithograph, *From the Boardwalk.* (fig. 2, il. 21). This correspondence plunges us further into the complex question of the relationship between the artist's photographs and his work in other media. *From the Boardwalk* is the only Kuniyoshi lithograph that is based directly on a photograph, but this unique example contradicts published accounts that deal specifically with this issue. Carl Zigrosser wrote perceptively about Kuniyoshi and photography in 1940:

> *His views on the use of photography by artists are interesting. He is an accomplished photographer and at one time made a living by photographing paintings for other artists. But he never makes use of photography in his creative work. He once made a lithograph from a photograph and after the edition was all printed he destroyed it, because it did not have the quality he sought. In this his instinct was sound, for the values emphasized by the camera lens are never those of the creative artist's vision. Kuniyoshi is ever sensitive to the inherent qualities of the medium, and keeps his lithography, painting, and photography separate, though each has enriched his experience as an artist.*[26]

The photographic source for the lithograph, *From the Boardwalk,* survives, although Zigrosser stated that the artist destroyed the lithographs that were based on a photograph. There is no doubt the artist was satisfied with his lithograph, because when the American Artists Congress held an exhibition of 100 prints simultaneously in 30 American cities, in December 1936, Kuniyoshi chose to exhibit *From the Boardwalk.*[27]

Kuniyoshi was reticent about the photographs he was making in the 1930s, a common attitude among painters at the time. This attitude was prompted by contemporary opinions that regarded photography as less artistic than painting—witness Zigrosser's statement that ". . . the values emphasized by the camera lens are never those of the creative artist's vision." Nevertheless, the visual evidence is irrefutable; in this instance Kuniyoshi based his lithograph on a photograph, and it provides a unique opportunity to compare his photography and his graphic art.

The photograph is the source of some of the details in Kuniyoshi's print, for example the feminine touch of a woman in the foreground wearing a handkerchief under her wristwatch. The photograph also rationalizes the improbable levitating foot of the second woman. But it is the changes Kuniyoshi made from the photograph that are most revealing. He places a newspaper under the hand of the foreground woman and puts a cigarette in her mouth, so she becomes a sister of the pensive woman he was painting in the 1930s.[28] By simplifying the composition and enlarging the scale of the figures he creates a space that seems closer to us and, giving the front woman a slight smile, he makes her seem pleasantly self-involved but accessible. The figures in the photograph do not smile or interact with each other; they are further away from our point of view, creating an image of greater detachment and psychological tension.

As Zigrosser wrote, "Kuniyoshi is ever sensitive to the inherent qualities of the medium." The photograph exploits its ability to represent contrasting textures, such as the smoothness of the girls' legs against the grainy sand. The lithograph attains its sensuality through traces of the movement of the lithographic crayon and the slight texture of ink on the thick paper. Ultimately there is a different sense of reality in the two works. No matter how much the photograph was cropped and manipulated we know—we can see—that it was originally made by mechanically recording the light and dark patterns of the real world on a piece of light-sensitive film. The light and dark patterns of the lithograph just as obviously have a manual origin, being drawn by hand on the lithographic stone. The difference in procedure gives the photograph a greater sense of objective reality, the lithograph a greater appearance of aesthetic manipulation.

In contrast to the vignetted lithograph, the rectangular format of the photograph is essential to its more complex composition. Kuniyoshi created a decentralized composition with a pair of feet in the top left corner, and two headless figures descending from the top edge. The partial figures give the picture the sense of a fragment selected from a more extensive scene, which the artist shot from above to create a modern, uptilted space. The incomplete figures and the unusual vantage point have a long artistic lineage, and are characteristic of many of Kuniyoshi's photographs, especially those of Coney Island.

Coney Island has been an inspiration to painters and photographers from the late 19th century to the present.[29] In the 1930s it was documented by both Kuniyoshi and his artist friend, Reginald Marsh. They had known each other since 1919, were pupils of Kenneth Hayes Miller at the Art Students League, and had studios near each other on 14th Street. Marsh started making photographs with his own 35mm Leica in 1938 (although he had already taken pictures in the early 1930s).[30] Like Kuniyoshi he took pictures of Union Square and of Coney Island. Their beach photographs differ consistently in one respect: Marsh's are generally taken straight-on, while Kuniyoshi usually shot his pictures from the boardwalk, looking down at the people on the beach. The space in Marsh's photographs, and in his paintings, conforms with traditional Western perspective, while Kuniyoshi presents us with a space both Oriental and modern.

Writing of the achievements of Degas and his contemporaries, Kirk Varnedoe has pointed out that after the 1870s,

Painting aggressively swung away from realist concerns into anti-naturalism; and the continuation of the Impressionist experiments with unorthodox concepts of space, time and point of view were redirected into far more insistently non-mimetic, expressive or decorative, languages of representation . . . Only much later, after the advent of the Leica and Surrealist thought, was serious attention again devoted, by photographers and filmmakers this time, to that line of modern Realist experiment that the painters of the 1870s began.[31]

Kuniyoshi serves as a fine example of Varnedoe's thesis. With his Japanese heritage and his admiration of the School of Paris, he was acutely aware of the influence of Oriental concepts of pictorial space on Degas. He told his students,

Degas learned a great deal from the Orientals. He had an extraordinary sense in constructing. He used big floor spaces, had faces half cut off.[32]

In Kuniyoshi's photograph, *Children, Coney Island* (fig. 4) a "floor" of sand takes up most of the space, and several figures have their heads cut off by the frame. The composition begins with the children walking in at the lower left corner, curves up through the reclining couple to the woman leaning against the box of garbage, and finally to the three truncated figures at the top left corner. Like Degas' *Place de la Concorde,* the center of the scene is void, an uptilted ground plane.[33] This dynamic, asymmetrical composition was created deliberately by Kuniyoshi, who cropped the negative precisely on three sides. This was one of the principal means of manipulation available to him, and we will see that it was common practice for him to strengthen the composition of his photographs by cropping their edges.

5. *Yasuo Kuniyoshi,* The Swimmer, *1924, oil on canvas, 20-1/8 × 30". Collection of Columbus Gallery of Fine Arts.*

6. *Reginald Marsh,* Boys Diving Off Pier. *c. 1938. Collection of the Museum of the City of New York.*

Another photograph of *Coney Island, Boardwalk and Bathers* (fig. 3) has fragments of figures at the top edge. Here Kuniyoshi has included a section of the boardwalk and its railing, which slices diagonally across the right side of the picture. Again Degas is the artist who inescapably comes to mind, both because of the aggressive disruption of continuous space by this diagonal plane, and because of the posture of the reclining woman on the sand below, who, paralleling the railing, establishes a visual harmony beween the two clashing planes.

One of Kuniyoshi's starkest pictures from the Coney Island series is his image of a solitary *Black Man on the Beach* (cover); a negative that he printed three times, twice in vertical format, once as a horizontal. It is a study of textures and densities, contrasting the firm, dark skin of the man and the malleable surface of the sand. The image of the inverted figure prone against a textured surface

finds an equivalent in Kuniyoshi's photograph of artist *Rosella Hartman Swimming* (fig. 6). Here we see a nude woman diagonally from above, floating in the water at Haines Falls, near Woodstock. The sand in the Coney Island pictures, a plane moving from the bottom to the top edge of the photograph while simultaneously tilting back into space, is here replaced by an expanse of water. Earlier paintings and drawings of bathers suspended against water, such as the *Swimmer* (il. 5) attest to Kunyoshi's long interest in the motif. The photographs, including *Boy Floating, Rockport, Mass.* (fig. 7) represents a continuing sensibility that again fuses French modernism with the Oriental spatial concepts that originally inspired the Parisians. The tilted wall of water can be found in Monet's *Water Lilies,*[34] and Kuniyoshi was explicit about his involvement with Japanese spatial construction in early paintings such as *Swimmer:*

> As a student I was taught to see things wide . . . but when I was on my own I got the idea to paint things looking down on them. Like Oriental. I didn't paint any sky—the ground slants up with all things on it.[35]

Kuniyoshi believed "each subject should be created according to the medium one chooses to deal with."[36] One property of the 35mm camera was its ability to capture the instant and he took advantage of this in his pictures of divers. Reginald Marsh took similar photographs of boys in the act of diving off a crowded pier, and a comparison reveals how the formal vision found in each artist's paintings is present in his photographs as well (il. 6, fig. 5). In his art Marsh consciously fused his twentieth-century New York environment with stylistic elements taken from Italian Renaissance painting. Consequently his photograph is seen frontally; the figures are upright, as are the architectural supports of the pier, which recedes in single-point perspective to the skyscrapers on the horizon. The left two-thirds of the picture are organized by a grid of beams. Kuniyoshi's simpler photograph has no grid and no horizon—it is dominated by a single diagonal set against a tilted plane of water. He took the photograph from well above the scene, to create a composition and space that derive from Japanese art and Impressionism, as opposed to the Renaissance tradition. By the mid-1930s, however, the use of the high vantage point was commonplace in photography, having been pioneered by photographers such as Lazlo Moholy-Nagy, Alexander Rodchenko, André Kertész, and Paul Strand, among others. Kuniyoshi was friendly with Berenice Abbott, who had been taking photographs of New York City streets from elevated viewpoints since at least 1929.[37] In his shots from above, Kuniyoshi was using a recent con-

vention of modern photography with great sensitivity. The high vantage point appears in a greater proportion of his photographs than in those by the photographers just mentioned. It seems a natural point of view for Kuniyoshi; the tilted-up space is shared by several of the pictorial traditions that meant the most to him—the Japanese, the French Modernist, and American folk-painting.

A correlate of the photographs from above is the view from below, and this is also found in Kunisyoshi's photographs. A series of pictures Konrad Cramer snapped of Kuniyoshi using his camera all show him crouching, which suggests this was a comfortable posture for the agile artist when photographing (frontispiece). Artist John Taylor, a friend of Kuniyoshi's in Woodstock, told a story that reveals Kuniyoshi's interest in capturing unusual points of view:

> He brought his camera along one day. We had a beautiful little grey cat, pure Maltese, not a spot of white, and she was quite a performer. I taught her by tying a little piece of paper on a string and swinging it up into the air so this little cat would go straight up into the air with its paws and grab at it. Yas thought that was great, very amused at things of this kind. So this was outside of the studio, so he lay on the ground on his back and the cat went up into the air and he snapped it. And Yas gave us a print of that, but it's been lost.[38]

When Kuniyoshi took one of his classes on a picnic to a lake surrounded by rocky cliffs, on a day in 1938, he used the cliffs to get a variety of unusual angles for his pictures. In *Boys Wrestling* (fig. 8) his low vantage point silhouettes the figures against the grey sky, creating a powerful image of a sport important in Japanese art and culture.

He simultaneously made use of views from above and below when he took his dazzling picture in the Glass Building of the 1939 World's Fair, photographing the high ceiling which was covered with mirrored tiles (fig. 9). The tiles form a rigid grid of squares that contrasts with the dramatic curve of the architecture, while reflecting the people below as if seen from far above. The random array of spectators plays against the regularity of the grid of mirrors, and each mirror reflects at slightly different angle from its neighbors', so the images of the spectators are fractured and staggered. The photograph is further complicated by arcs of light on the floor and the light fixtures on the ceiling that curve through the composition. These fixtures are seen from far below, right next to the tops of the heads of the spectators reflected from far above. Kuniyoshi recognized the aesthetic potential of the mir-

7. *Yasuo Kuniyoshi,* Sara Reading, *1938, photograph, 7-1/4 × 9-1/2". Collection of Sara M. Kuniyoshi.*

8. *Yasuo Kuniyoshi,* I'm Tired, *1938, oil on canvas, 40-1/4 × 31". Collection of Whitney Museum of American Art.*

rored ceiling, which combines two unusual vantage points in one complex scene, and he produced one of his richest photographs, with the image of himself taking it hidden within it.

In contrast, a photograph of the artist's wife, Sara, seated at a table smoking and reading *Life* magazine seems uninspired and undistinguished (il. 7). It is, however, closely related to Kunyoshi's contemporary paintings of lone women brooding over their newspapers;[39] perhaps he was curious to see how his photographic version would compare to his painted ones. The Whitney Museum's *I'm Tired* (1938, il. 8) is closest to the photograph in subject and date. As in many of these comparisons, the specificity of the photograph has its appeal, but the painterly handling, the color, and the more generalized quality of the painting seem truer to Kuniyoshi's artistic aims: "I have never really painted a portrait of anybody . . . I paint universal woman . . ."[40] However, when he took advantage of the mobility afforded him by his "miniature" camera and photographed the same scene from an unconventional point of view, the result is original and compelling (fig. 10). The image of Sara calmly leaning forward with objects hovering inexplicably around her and nothing seeming to support her weight is startling and confusing. Eventually we realize that the photographer has positioned himself underneath the glass table, looking up through it at her, and has transformed a commonplace scene into an arresting visual experience.

This picture of Sara Kuniyoshi is only one of many fascinating images of women found among Kuniyoshi's photographs, as we might expect from an artist who constantly painted and drew women. They appear in a greater variety of roles and moods in his photographs than in his paintings. Although the pair of waitresses linking arms in the painting, *Two Waitresses from Sparhawk* (1924-5) looks forward to the feminine comradery Kuniyoshi captured in his photograph, *St. John's Daughters* (1937, fig. 13), in general the speed and flexibility of photography encouraged him to convey a wider range of attitudes with his camera than with his brush. His photograph of *Andrée Ruellan and Elsie Speicher* (fig. 12) contrasts a slender, delicate woman with a matronly, pompous one in typology that recalls the caricatures of Daumier, one of Kuniyoshi's favorite artists.[41] A more serious mood comes from the juxtaposition of *Sara and Inez* (fig. 11), a profound dialogue of gestures and expressions that hints at the traditional theme of the active versus the contemplative life.

His photographs of *Nudes* continue the mood of subdued melancholy found in many of his works of the late

9. *Yasuo Kuniyoshi,* Morris Kantor, *1938, photograph, 6-5/8 × 9-1/4". Collection of Sara M. Kuniyoshi.*

1930s. He photographed them in natural sunlight in his studio, creating stronger contrasts of values than usual in his work. He captures a mood of reverie by photographing the model's head in shadow with her eyes averted from our gaze (fig. 14). Other pictures, like *Torso* (fig. 15), are more explicitly sexual, but abstracted by being only partial figures. These isolated torsos have no parallel in Kuniyoshi's paintings. The figure fragment was an established tradition in modern sculpture, however, and Kuniyoshi had personal contact with it: he had acquired a small *Torso* from sculptor Gaston Lachaise in the 1920s in exhange for a painting. Imogen Cunningham and Edward Weston were among many photographers who isolated parts of the female body in their works of the 1920s. These works seem mild today, but they were considered racy in the pre-*Playboy* years. One of the few photographs that Kuniyoshi published was *Nude* (fig. 16) which appeared in the 1937 *Leica Annual*.[42] The volume is full of well-mannered portraits, pictures of machines, men at work, and flowers. It is still a surprise to turn the page and see the only nude in the book reduced to a pair of voluptuous breasts. Kuniyoshi may have included the photograph as a joke; it would have been a deliberately outrageous joke since, in the same year, one of his paintings of a nude was removed from an exhibition at the University of Wyoming.[43]

The photograph of painter *Morris Kantor* (fig. 17) introduces a grotesque mood that has parallels in all phases of Kuniyoshi's art. Kantor, a fellow teacher at the Art Students League, had a studio near Kuniyoshi's on 14th Street in the late 1920s. He gazes urbanely out of the photograph, while leaning with his elbow on a partially

draped mannequin. The mannequin was a standard prop of the Surrealists from their precursor, de Chirico, to the late Surrealist, Hans Bellmer, and his *poupée*. Kuniyoshi here uses the dummy's awkward, inanimate eroticism to impart an air of decadent sophistication to the mustachioed Kantor. Typically, he cropped the negative on all sides, centralizing and monumentalizing the composition of two leaning figures linked by the arch of the sofa's back. (il. 9).

The mannequin also appears in Kuniyoshi's disconcerting painting, *Lay Figure* (1937-8, il. 27), with more drapery and a newspaper, but in almost the same pose. Kuniyoshi has created a bizarre, anthropomorphic still life where the mannequin leans precariously across a wicker chair. The painting's animated drawing, eloquent color, painterly touch, and large size make it more imposing than the photograph. Both works share a macabre mood, but the photograph has the power of veracity, presenting a stylish image of an artist posing for his picture in 1938.

Kuniyoshi's fondness for American folk art led him to place a wooden carousel horse in the backyard of his house in Woodstock. He photographed the horse in profile, silhouetted against the sky and Overlook Mountain (fig. 18). The horse is supported by the post below it, but the way its hooves barely touch the hedge that forms the bottom zone of the composition makes it seem to skim through the air. Kuniyoshi again combines a folk sensibility with a lyrical fantasy, as he had done in early paintings.

In photographs like *Morris Kantor* and *Carousel Horse* the artist seems to delight in subverting the documentary realism of the medium by suggesting feelings of the bizarre or the fantastic. Straight realism is again

10. Ben Shahn, May Day Parade, *1935, photograph. Collection of the Fogg Art Museum, Harvard University.*

cheerfully negated in *Fun House Mirror* (1938, fig. 19). The backs of the heads of several school girls occupy the bottom of the composition, which is dominated by their smiling, mishapened reflections in a distorting mirror. The stretched-out girls, presided over by a genial, squashed matron at the top, loom over the "real" heads in the foreground as if the warped ones were about to take over.

In one of his most memorable photographs, *May Day Parade* (1937, fig. 20), Kuniyoshi turns his taste for the grotesque to an image that crystallizes the political mood of the late 1930s, when the liberal community in the United States was a horrified spectator as fascist dictators manipulated world history. In the midst of a realistic crowd scene on 14th Street, Hitler and Mussolini, with huge, scowling heads, look towards the spectator. Mussolini waves one awkward hand while Hitler clutches his puppet, Francesco Franco. They grimace at a young man who looks in at them from the left edge of the photograph. He is a fragment, an anonymous spectator who stands in for us, confronting this horrific trio.

The May Day parade was an annual left-wing demonstration that ended in Union Square, near Kuniyoshi's studio. Japan's invasion of Manchuria in 1931 had politicized Kuniyoshi, who later worked actively against Japanese militarism in World War II.[44] In 1935 he was a founding member of the American Artist Congress whose motto was, "Against War and Facism."[45] *The New York Times* described the 1937 May Day parade as, "united on one dominating slogan of the day, which was to help the democracy of Spain fight Fascism,"[46] and Kuniyoshi was sympathetic to the mood of the demonstration when he took his photograph.

Comparable photographs of the 1935 May Day Parade were taken by Ben Shahn (il. 10), a friend of Kuniyoshi's and another painter-photographer. His photographs record the Artist's Union part of the parade in a documentary, photojournalistic manner. For example, one picture shows a crowd scene with rows of chanting demonstrators advancing towards the photographer. In contrast to Shahn's realist style, two years later Kuniyoshi, with his eye for the fantastic, created a bizarre allegory of the world situation.

Other Kuniyoshi photographs are more conventionally Social Realist. *Fish Market* (1938, fig.21) shows men pouring barrels of fish into the back of a truck, manual laborers in the machine age. A trip to the South in 1939 resulted in several noble images of Southern blacks, a racially and economically repressed class. The photograph of two Negro couples (fig. 22), monumentalized by the way they rise above the straight horizon,

especially expresses this dignity; Kuniyoshi sympathized with victims of racial discrimination as he had experienced it himself.

In a speech given at the Museum of Modern Art in February, 1940, entitled "What Is American in American Art," Kuniyoshi said,

> All creative work is colored by the immediate environment. When you hear the clang of fire engines; shuffle through the subways; rush by heaps of automobile wrecks; push your way through the crowd on Main Street—all these things temper and shape the American, no matter where the individual first came from.[47]

His own immediate environment alternated between upstate New York and New York City, and he recorded both areas with his camera. In the late 1930s he executed landscapes in many media inspired by scenes he saw upstate, and they share the pre-war melancholy of his figurative pieces. Artist Karl Fortess remembers going with Kuniyoshi on a fruitful sketching and photographing trip to an abandoned brickmaking factory on Glasco Turnpike near East Kingston, New York. It resulted in a group of photographs, drawings, and the painting, *Deserted Brickyard* (1938, il. 11). Kuniyoshi photographed this scene, but we have only his negatives, no prints—apparently he considered it suitable for a painting but not a photograph. Fortess feels that "The sketching trips were basically for getting information. That's why he took his camera along, to gather information."[48] But it was information that he edited considerably to get a finished print. We can see, comparing a photograph from their trip, *East Kingston* (fig. 23), with its negative (il. 12), that Kuniyoshi cut out about one-fourth of the negative, cropping it on all sides to purify the image into a near-abstact composition of contrasting angles and textures.

This print typifies one extreme of Kuniyoshi's photographic expression, his interest in formal beauty, which can be seen again in his close-up view of *Abandoned Woodshed* (fig. 25). An expanse of jagged horizontal boards becomes a rich texture study, while the shallow space and the thin white lines drawn against the wood grain recall the artist's own love of drawing. When he pulls back from the woodshed for a larger view (fig. 24), the stark geometries become more evocative. The skeletal ruin in the photograph embodies this air of desolation as do Kuniyoshi's drawings of the same theme.[49]

As with the close-up of *Abandoned Woodshed*, in some of his urban photographs Kuniyoshi combines the documentary nature of photography with formal concerns that parallel the painterly and compositional issues found

in his paintings. His fourth floor studio at 30 East 14th Street made it easy for him to take pictures from above, creating the up-tilted space discussed in relation to his Coney Island photographs. In *Union Square* (fig. 26) we again find a central void framed by diagonals, with objects cut off by the picture's edge. The co-existence of the automobile with the horse-drawn wagon pinpoints a specific period in the development of twentieth-century car culture. Again Kuniyoshi has fused the factuality of the camera with compositional ideas derived from French modernism and his own Oriental heritage. His description of Degas' method can be applied neatly to his own photographs:

> Degas for example borrowed the basic construction and theory of Japanese composition. He adapted it to conform with his own environment and obtained an individual expression.[50]

In three of his pictures of Union Square taken from his studio window (fig. 28) Kuniyoshi came close to recreating his ideals as a painter in the medium of photography, although thematically these pictures have nothing in common with his works in other media. His paintings of the 1930s are characterized by his subtle and sensual paint handling, along with his elegant control of

11. Yasuo Kuniyoshi, Deserted Brickyard, *1938, oil on canvas, 20-1/8 × 35-1/4". Collection of Honolulu Academy of Arts. Gift of Mrs. Philip E. Spalding.*

12. Yasuo Kuniyoshi, East Kingston, *1938, photograph, copy print from original negative. Collection of Sara M. Kuniyoshi.*

subdued colors and close values. In most of the photographs Kuniyoshi printed he expressed this painterly sensibility by using a matte surface and playing down value contrasts. Sara Kuniyoshi recalls that he hated high contrast in his photographs.

Nowhere is the painterliness of Kuniyoshi's photographs more apparent than in *Union Square in the Snow* (fig. 27). Recalling Monet and Pissarro, he recorded his urban environment with a picture of a snow scene from above. The composition is dominated in the foreground by a broad V that is closed by a horizontal line sweeping across the top of the picture, creating an upside-down triangle, an inversion of the Renaissance ideal of a broad-based, pyramidal composition. The snow renders most of the scene white and the elevated vantage point tilts the space up, so the photograph becomes analogous to a canvas or a sheet of paper. The malleability of the snow creates a tactile field, so that the dark band of car tracks across the top of the scene looks as soft as a line of paint dragged across a canvas by a loaded brush. The interwoven car tracks at the bottom of the photograph are drawn in the white snow with a softness that suggests charcoal on paper. Kuniyoshi has created an extraordinarily painterly image that retains the factuality of photography—it is a picture of Union Square at a specific instant on a specific winter day in 1939. The snow blurs all details so that nothing stands out sharply in the manner that Kuniyoshi found objectionable in photographs:

> He talked quite a bit about photography in relation to painting, and said that to him a photograph was something entirely different from a painting and that he just could not use photographs in his work. He said that in a photograph one part would be clear and precise and the background would be all soft and out of focus; whereas in his painting he wanted everything to be sharp and clear, even though the different planes might be very close in tone and color.[51]

These remarks, recorded by Lloyd Goodrich in 1948, are among the few observations on photography by Kuniyoshi that have been preserved for us. The artist, whose camera was described in 1937 as, "the almost constant companion of his leisure hours,"[52] seems to have been both attracted to the medium and sceptical of it. In 1940, remembering the first Western painting he saw as a boy in Japan, a realistic battle scene, he wrote:

> It stirred me greatly because it was so real and lifelike, a factor that I had not been aware of in the works of art that surrounded my childhood . . . As I look back, no doubt it was a very photographic depiction; however, the approach and medium strange-

> ly moved me and has left an impression vivid to this day. It may not be that the memory of this picture was responsible for my becoming an artist but it has remained as a symbol of my aims; to combine the rich traditions of the East with my accumulative experiences and viewpoint of the West.[53]

A 1942 article on Kuniyoshi's activities during World War II, in *The New Yorker,* concluded:

> So far he has had no unpleasant scenes with patriotic people he bumps into on the street. The only real hardship he has suffered is that he can't pursue his hobby, which is, as you might know, photography. He won a third prize at the Leica exhibition four years ago. The cops have taken his camera for the duration.[54]

In his 1948 discussions with Lloyd Goodrich, Kuniyoshi repeatedly said that he took photographs "for his own pleasure."[55]

Although Kuniyoshi had been a professional photographer of works of art in the 1920s, he considered his later photography a hobby, something done for his own enjoyment. We have seen that it was a hobby he pursued actively in the late 1930s, taking and printing over 400 photographs. But his main interest was painting, and as his last dated photograph is from 1939 we must assume that he abandoned photography of his own will at least a year before he had to surrender his camera in late 1941. In 1939 he had his first one-man exhibition in three years, an exhibition that solidified his reputation as an important American painter. He received awards for his paintings and was active in several artist's groups.[56] Not only was he very busy, but photography's status as an art form was a controversial subject.

Painters who used photographs in their work were suspect, although Reginald Marsh made no secret of using his photographs as sources, and a dialogue between painting and photography was the basis of much of Charles Sheeler's art. Despite the heroic efforts of Alfred Stieglitz to establish photography as art, the topic was still a volatile one in the 1930s. Sara Kuniyoshi recalls that when Kuniyoshi was the first president of Artists Equity, from 1947 to 1951, "The quarrel was whether to admit photographers or not . . . I think Paul Strand finally made it." When Charles Sheeler wanted to exhibit his photographs in a show at the Downtown Gallery (Kuniyoshi's Gallery), dealer Edith Halpert would not allow it.[57] Clearly, the subject of photography was controversial, at a time when graver political pressures were mounting for Kuniyoshi. In addition, he knew people like Alfred Stieglitz, Berenice Abbott, Barbara and Willard Morgan,

13. Yasuo Kuniyoshi, Summer Storm, *1938, oil on canvas, 26 × 38-1/4". Collection of Detroit Institute of Arts. Gift of Dr. and Mrs. George Kamperman*

14. Yasuo Kuniyoshi, Horse, *c. 1922, photograph, 8 × 10", Collection of Sara M. Kuniyoshi.*

who were devoting their careers to photography with a seriousness and a commitment that Kuniyoshi reserved for his paintings.

These are the factors that we surmise led Kuniyoshi to abandon photography. They also may explain his reticence about his photographs. But he carefully saved them, either mounted or in labelled and dated folders, and they are rewarding to look at today. The strength of his best photographs is due to his eye: the visual way he selected his subjects and compositions. We have endeavored to demonstrate that the sensibility that made Kuniyoshi one of the leading painters of his time carries into his photographs, and that knowledge about his photography gives us new insights into his paintings. The photographs complement the rest of Kuniyoshi's art. They also stand as original and beautiful creations in their own right.

* * *

The story of Kuniyoshi and photography has a denouncement, and it is found in his paintings. We have

15. Yasuo Kuniyoshi, My Man, 1943, casein on board, 14-11/16 × 10-1/2",
The Art Institute of Chicago. Olivia Shaler Swan Collection.

seen how his involvement with picturef taking was herald-
ed by his inclusion of images of photographs in his still-life
paintings. He continued this practice through the 1930s.
In Things on Iron Chair (1939, il. 23) he depicted a group
of bent and folded objects on an ornate chair, the
assembly dominated by a Mexican jug. Squeezed between
the jug and the chair's back is a folded painting—a still life
within a still life. It was a canvas of his that he was
dissatisfied with, so he unstretched it and incorporated it
into another painting. The jug stands in front of this still
life, on top of a scarf that partially covers a grey and white
rectangle. After some scrutiny, the rectangle reveals itself
to be a boxing scene: a bent-over fighter is on the left, with

only his opponent's leg visible to the right; the rest is
overlapped b the scarf. The boxing scene looks like a
sports photo—and indeed it is, for the actual picture is still
in the Kuniyoshi estate (il. 24).[58] Earlier, the artist painted
reproductions of Old Masters into his still lifes, now he has
used an anonymous contemporary photograph. He
painted Things on Iron Chair directly from the objects: he
photographed his set-up next to the painting (il. 17), and it
reveals that the assembling of the subject was a key step in
the creation of a still-life painting for Kuniyoshi.

A 1938 painting continues the series of still lifes with
images within them, But here Kuniyoshi relieves any ambiguity with his title: Photograph and Peaches on Chair, so

we know we are looking at a painting of a photograph (il. 20). Now it is a large photograph of a nude woman wrapping herself in a fur, a paraphrase of Ruben's *Het Pélskin*, which Kuniyoshi owned in photographic reproduction. By the time of this painting he was actively involved with making his own photographs—the clip hanging on the corner of the photograph in the painting refers to his techniques of drying his photographs, just as the sketchbook on the chair refers to his techniques of drawing.

In the early 1940's the horse was a recurrent symbol for Kuniyoshi in a series of paintings that expressed his distress at world conditions. In *Summer Storm* (1938, il. 13) he adopted an emotional theme that was popular among Romantic painters of the early nineteenth century: a frightened horse in a storm. He painted the agitated horse from a photograph, in this case one of his own, from the days in the 1920's when he was an art photographer and took a picture of an Oriental ceramic horse (il. 14).[59]

Several important Kuniyoshi paintings from the 1940's rephrase themes he had already explored in his photographs: *Deserted Stone Quarry* (1943) continues his desolate industrial landscapes, while *My Man* (1943, il. 15) returns to Coney Island, and to the reclining horse is also continued, but the lyricism of Kuniyoshi's *Carousel Horse* photograph (fig. 18) is replaced by a mood of anguished dislocation. *Festivities Ended* was finished in 1947, but begun in 1939, the year Kuniyoshi's photography ended. In the painting the carousel horse is upside-down, skewered by its post, in front of a barren landscape of dead bodies. A wooden horse appears again in *Headless Horse Who Wants to Jump* (1945, il. 16), with a similar mood of pessimism.

Kuniyoshi's incorporation of photographs into his still lifes continues in a new way in a painting he made in 1942, after he relinquished his camera. *End of Juanita* (il. 31) is a rephrasing of *Things on Iron Chair* six years later. It includes the same jug and a similar discarded still-life painting. But the boxing scene from the earlier painting has been replaced by a photograph of a nude woman with her arms raised. For the first time, the image within the painting is based on one of his own photographs (il. 32), and it represents something abandoned, like the painting below it.

Two years after *End of Juanita*, Kuniyoshi painted *Broken Objects* (1944, il. 34), a still life about destruction. Painted with his characteristic luscious, warm colors, an eccentric assembly of shattered and fragmented things is surrounded by expansive space, so they seem small and vulnerable. Again, the artist included one of his own photographs in his painting, once more a nude (fig. 16).

16. Anonymous, Headless Horse Who Wants to Jump, 1945, photograph of studio set-up, 9-3/8 × 7-1/2. Collection of Sara M. Kuniyoshi.

The photograph has been torn in two. The jug, now broken, separates the pieces, and the ripped photograph joins the other destroyed objects in a mournful scene that quietly reflects Kuniyoshi's, and the world's despair in 1944.

Kuniyoshi's still lifes are some of his most personal paintings. Speaking of these works, he said,

> I picked up all kind of materials—cigars and toys and weathervanes and the old sofa in Woodstock, where I was going then. I picked them for shapes, colors, textures—but sometimes when they were all together they take on symbolism for me.[60]

His class monitor from the early 1940s remembers that when she asked Kuniyoshi who the best contemporary painters in the various genres were, he began "For still-life painters—me."[61] While he was secretive about his photographs, he was proud of his still lifes. They are some of his most significant paintings, and the following essay by Bruce Weber represents the first serious attempt to unravel their complex meanings.

FOOTNOTES

All unnoted quotations and biographical information were taken from conversations with Sara Mazo Kuniyoshi in Woodstock and New York City between March 1982 and June 1983. This project would not have been possible without her dedicated and discriminating participation. The hard work and enthusiastic collaboration of Bruce Weber and Linda Weintraub were also essential to the success of this exhibition and essay.

1. Immigration Act of 1924.

2. New York *World Telegram,* February 23, 1940.

3. Interview with Anne Helioff Hirschberg, Woodstock, May 30, 1983. Mrs. Hirschberg was Kuniyoshi's class monitor during the war.

4. The War Powers Act of 1941 impounded all Japanese money in U.S. banks. Isidor Glasdal, Kuniyoshi's lawyer, wrote him on December 13, 1941, "As to the release of your impounded funds, that is a matter that will have to wait for the promulgation of regulations of the Treasury Department . . ." Kuniyoshi's funds still had not been released by the following summer, and he was forced to open a painting school in Woodstock. To make space for the students in his studio he dismantled his dark room. All letters cited are in the collection of Sara Kuniyoshi.

5. Kuniyoshi to the U.S. Attorney, New York City, January 2, 1942; "I read in today's paper of the regulation requiring me to notify your office of any proposed trip . . ."

6. Isidor Glasgal to Mathias Correa, U.S. District Attorney, January 5, 1942; "Mr. Kuniyoshi, who is an enemy alien, has complied with the regulation requiring the delivery of small cameras and radios to the police department." Kuniyoshi's friend, Karl Fortess, remembered that Kuniyoshi was allowed to transfer the ownership of his camera to him at the police station. Interview, September 25, 1982.

7. Biographical data from *Yasuo Kuniyoshi 1889-1953,* University of Texas at Austin, 1975, p. 9-14. The basic text on Kuniyoshi is Lloyd Goodrich, *Yasuo Kuniyoshi,* Whitney Museum of American Art, 1948.

8. Lloyd Goodrich, "Katherine Schmidt" in *The Katherine Schmidt Shubert Bequest and A Selective View of Her Art,* Whitney Museum of American Art, 1982, p. 6.

9. Yasuo Kuniyoshi, "East to West", *Magazine of Art,* 33, February 1940, p. 77.

10. Alexander Brook, "Yasuo Kuniyoshi—A Tribute," in *Yasuo Kuniyoshi 1889-1953. op. cit.,* p. 54. Kuniyoshi's camera was a Korona 8 x 10 with a Goertz Dogmar variable diffusion lens. Our thanks to Howard Greenberg for this information and for his assistance in innumerable other ways.

11. Kuniyoshi's stamp, "Kuniyoshi 110 Columbia Hgts. Brooklyn, NY. Phone Main 2649 " appears on the back of a photograph, in Sara Kuniyoshi's collection, of El Greco's *View of Toledo.* The painting was bequeathed to the Metropolitan Museum of Art in 1929 by Mrs. Havemeyer.

12. Dorothea Greenbaum collection, Princeton, N.J.

13. Museum of Modern Art.

14. Henry McBride, "Modern Art," *The Dial,* 78, March 1925, p. 255.

15. Forbes Watson, review, January 11, 1925, clipping book in collection of Sara Kuniyoshi.

16. Kuniyoshi, "East to West," *op. cit., p. 80.*

17. Prado Museum.

18. Kuniyoshi loaned a folk painting of a train to a 1924 exhibition at the Whitney Studio Club, the first exhibition of folk art held at an American museum. An illustration of this painting, photographed by Charles Sheeler, appears in the pamphlet that accompanied the exhibition. Juliana Force and Henry Schnakenberg, organizers, *Early American Art,* Whitney Studio Club, 1924.

19. Interview, Rosella Hartman Fiene, Woodstock, October 14, 1982.

20. An interpretation of this painting that anticipates ours appears in, Donald J. Bear, "Santa Barbara Muralist Accorded Tribute in Review of New Trends—Kuniyoshi Still-life in Museum also Applauded," *Santa Barbara News Press,* clipping book, collection Sara Kuniyoshi.

21. Atsuo Imaizumi and Lloyd Goodrich, *Kuniyoshi: Catalogue of Kuniyoshi's Posthumous Exhibition,* National Museum of Modern Art, Tokyo, pl. 12 ex-collection Jean Mauzé.

22. On loan to the San Francisco Museum of Modern Art.

23. Pitti Palace, Florence.

24. David Rosand, *Titian,* Harry N. Abrams, New York, 1978, p. 106.

25. Jacob Deschin, "How the Leica Changed Photography," *Leica Manual, The Complete Book of 35mm Photography,* Morgan & Morgan, Hastings-on-Hudson, 1973, New York, p. 421-6.

26. Carl Zigrosser, "The Prints of Yasuo Kuniyoshi," *Parnassus,* 12, 1940, p. 21.

27. American Artists Congress, *America Today: A Book of 100 Prints,* 1936, reprinted by DaCapo Press as *Graphic Works of the American 30s,* 1977, p. 5-6, pl. 45. Kuniyoshi was on the jury for this show; each of the thirteen jurors was asked to include one of his own works in the exhibition. Zigrosser's account is repeated by Van Deren Coke in his important survey, *The Painter and the Photograph,* Albuquerque, University of New Mexico Press, 1964, p. 300. There is evidence that Kuniyoshi based a lithograph on a photograph and then destroyed it when he was in Paris in 1928—see Lloyd Goodrich's notes from a conversation with Kuniyoshi, Archives of American Art (Roll M670 55WMP).

28. In *Daily News* (1935, The Cincinnati Art Museum) the musing woman holds a newpaper and a cigarette; the hat behind her suggests an unseen male presence, as the shoes do in *From the Boardwalk.*

29. Samuel S. Carr's painting, *The Beach at Coney Island* (c.1879) shows a family having its picture taken on the beach by a portrait photographer. See John Wilmerding, Linda Ayres, and Earl A. Powell, *An American Perspective—Nineteenth Century Art from the Colllection of Jo Ann & Julian Ganz,* Washington, National Gallery of Art, 1981, p. 54, 56, 121. Those who have taken photographs at Coney Island include Walker Evans, Weegee, and Eve Sonneman.

30. Reginald Marsh, July 20, 1938 entry in his photo record book: "1st film developed & taken by myself printed according to Leica Manual." The film was taken at Coney Island. Reginald Marsh Archive, Museum of the City of New York. See also, Norman Sasowsky, *Reginald Marsh—Photographs of New York,* Middendorf Gallery and the Reginald Marsh Estate, 1977; a limited edition portfolio of 25 plus 4 artists proofs, copy at Art Students League, New York.

31. J. Kirk T. Varnedoe, "The Artifice of Candor: Impressionism and Photography Reconsidered," *Art in America,* 68, January 1980, p. 76.

32. Mary Meixner, "Yasuo Kuniyoshi Talks with Students," *College Art Journal, 13, no. 1, Fall 1953,* p. 14.

33. Kuniyoshi owned a copy of Ambrose Vollard's *Degas, An Intimate Portrait,* trans. Randolph T. Weaver, New York, Greenberg Publisher Inc., 1927. *Place de la Concorde* is illustrated on page 97.

34. Monet's paintings are specifically suggested by Kuniyoshi's photograph, *Water Lily,* one of the few of his photographs to be published during his life. It is in Willard D. Morgan and Henry Lester, *Leica Manual, 2nd ed., Morgan and Lester, Publishers, New York, 1936,* p. 9.

35. Aline B. Louchheim, "Kuniyoshi: look, my past," *Art News,* 47, no. 2, April 1948, p. 47.

36. Yasuo Kuniyoshi, Talk given at the Albany Institute during the 1930's, Archives of American Art (Roll M676 121 WMP).

37. Kuniyoshi and Abbott were fellow members of the American Artists Congress during the period he was making photographs. He owned one of her photographs, and Sara Kuniyoshi recalls that he shared her enthusiasm for the work of Eugène Atget. Kuniyoshi owned *Atget, Photographe de Paris,* preface by Pierre MacOrlan, U.S. ed., Weyhe, New York, 1930.

38. Interview, John Taylor and Andrée Ruellan, Shady, New York, September 26, 1982. On this occasion, as in the past, Mr. Taylor and Ms. Ruellan were informative, gracious, and generous in helping us with our research, and we deeply regret the death of John Taylor.

39. These begin with *Quiet Thought* in 1932 (col. Mrs. David Milton) and conclude with *Season Ended,* 1940-45 (col. Mr. Edwin D. Levinson), but the bulk of Kuniyoshi's paintings on this theme are clustered in the years he was taking photographs. These include *Daily News,* 1935; *Picking a Horse,* 1937 (col. Mrs. Burton Tremaine); *Waiting,* 1938 (Israel Museum); *All Alone,* 1938; (ex. Downtown Gallery), and *I Think So,* 1939, (Albright-Knox Gallery).

40. Yasuo Kuniyoshi, "Universality in Art," typescript collection Sara Kuniyoshi, p. 2.

41. Daumier was among the artists whose photographs Kuniyoshi set on the bookshelves in his Woodstock house, along with Corot, Courbet, Delacroix, Eakins, Matisse, Picasso, Renoir, Toulouse-Lautrec.

42. Henry Lester, ed., *Leica 1937 Photo Annual,* Morgan and Lester, Publishers, New York, November, 1936, pl. 124.

43. "The Fig Leaf has now come to the University Campus." *The Nation, 142, March 18, 1936.*

44. He made posters for the Office of War Information and gave two speeches broadcast to Japan on February 10 and March 12, 1942; typescripts collection of Sara Kuniyoshi.

45. See Victoria Hoffman's Senior Project, The American Artists Congress, Bard College, May 1983.

46. The New York Times, Sunday, May 2, 1937.

47. Yasuo Kuniyoshi, "What Is American In American Art," speech given at the Musum of Modern Art, typescript, col. Sara Kuniyoshi.

48. Fortess, op. cit.

49. Kuniyoshi said that he "tried to get the idea of emptiness and sadness" in his landscapes of the late 1930s and 1940s. Louchheim, *op. cit., p. 55.*

50. Kuniyoshi, "What Is American In American Art," *op. cit.*

51. Lloyd Goodrich, conversation with Yasuo Kuniyoshi, Archives of American Art (Reel M670 62WMP). Kuniyoshi's concerns recall late 19th century painterly photographers. Alfred Stieglitz experimented with the abstracting qualities of snow and with urban scenes viewed from above in *From My Window, New York* (1902).

52. Harry Salpeter, "Yasuo Kuniyoshi: Artists' Artists," *Esquire,* April, 1937, p. 73.

53. Kuniyoshi, "East to West," *op. cit., p. 73.*

54. " 'Telling Tokio,' The Talk of the Town," *The New Yorker, 18, March 28, 1942,* p. 17.

55. Goodrich, Archives of American Art, *op. cit.*

56. Kuniyoshi's prizes and offices in these years included, First prize, American section, Golden Gate International Exposition, San Francisco, 1939-40; Second prize, 37th Annual International Exhibition of Paintings, Carnegie Institute, 1939; Vice-President of the American Artists Congress, 1938-40; President of An American Group, 1939-44.

57. Beaumont Newhall in a telephone conversation with Arnold Newman, reported to the authors, May 24, 1983.

58. Kuniyoshi also included a newspaper image of boxers, in *Odd Objects on Couch,* 1930, (Phila. Museum of Art).

59. The Oriental horse photograph bearing Kuniyoshi's photographer stamp, was in Kuniyoshi's file cabinet in a folder labelled *Summer Storm.*

60. Louchheim, *op. cit., p. 47.*

61. Hirschberg, *op. cit.*

*17. Yasuo Kuniyoshi, Things on Iron Chair and Studio Set-up,
1939, photograph, 7-1/2 × 9-1/2". Collection of Sara M. Kuniyoshi.*

Yasuo Kuniyoshi's Symbolic Still Lifes: Mind at Work

by Bruce Weber

At mid-career the Japanese-American artist Yasuo Kuniyoshi (1889-1953), created a group of mystifying still life paintings which expressed his personal and artistic experience and philosophy. Several received distinguished awards, and helped establish his reputation as one of America's leading artists. Lloyd Goodrich remarked that "Kuniyoshi's still lifes were the expression of delight in the physical properties of objects . . . These still-lifes always seemed more than an assemblage of inanimate objects; they contained an element of symbolism, a suggestion of something beyond the things themselves."[1]

In his major still lifes of the period 1933-1945, Kuniyoshi used common objects of everyday life as well as those which reflected his artistic outlook and personal taste, seeking to imbue them with a heightened sense of reality. The arrangements he used were small in scale in comparison to the finished picture (il. 17). He believed that the sum of the parts had the capacity to induce a state of mind that was different than when the objects were represented individually. As Kuniyoshi wrote:

When I walk out on the street, if I see anything interesting in shape and color, even stones, I pick them up and bring them home. If I see an interesting antique in a window I go in and buy it. I gather together all these materials and gradually I get used to them until they are a part of me. When I am thoroughly acquainted with these objects I fit them together to suit my feeling and construct material for a still life. I know exactly what it is all about because I have felt it. Because I love it, because I feel the truth, and truth is not an actuality, truth is knowledge of an object from within.[2]

The notion of transformation or metamorphosis was central to Kuniyoshi's mature aesthetic point of view. By 1933, he felt he had gone too far in the "direction of reality," that he "must combine thought with reality [and] use the object to start then discard it sufficiently to paint the superimposed idea."[3]

Kuniyoshi began to construct elaborate still life set-ups, believing that in starting a still life it was important to compose it as definitively and completely as possible, even if it took him several days to do so. Next he would

study it and make a careful drawing of it on the canvas, and perhaps start painting it from reality. But then he does not paint it anymore; he keeps it in the studio to look at sometimes, or he studies individual objects; but he does not paint actually from the objects when he gets into the picture . . . the picture becomes the important thing .[4]

Once involved in actually painting, Kuniyoshi became involved in evoking a message:

meaning . . . is important . . . It isn't the shape or color but much broader . . . [the] very thing of hidden meaning . . . Although it may change as [it] goes on . . . generalized idea of . . . meaning in the painting should be carried out . . . Sometimes . . . play with it, romanticize it . . . shift it in many directions, as time goes on.[5]

Still life now became a means of taking "something from reality . . . and from there all philosophy and life enters in. A painting is your idea of your life and experience."[6]

Occasional mention has been made by American art historians of Surrealist overtones in Kuniyoshi's art of the 1930s and 1940s. Yet his art rarely adopted the impossible, Freudian-based subjects and semi-abstract methods of Surrealism. Kuniyoshi's still lifes were more likely affected by an awareness of Metaphysical and Magic Realist art. In terms of the actual types and combinations of objects, they bear comparison to works by Giorgio de Chirico (1888-1978), Carlo Carra (1881-1966), and Filippo de Pisis (1896-1956). Closer to home, Kuniyoshi's mature still lifes recall the work of the Magic Realist Lorser Feitelson (1898-1978). Rather than describing them as Surrealistic, Metaphysical, or Magic Realist, perhaps it would be proper to adopt Feitelson's general term Post-Surrealist.

18. *Yasuo Kuniyoshi,* Weathervane and Other Objects, *1933,*
oil on canvas, 35-1/4 × 60-1/8". Collection of Santa Barbara Museum of Art. Gift of Wright Lundington.

Art is the subject of Kuniyoshi's *Weathervane and Other Objects,* which was originally titled *Sculpture Mold and Other Objects* (il. 18).[7] It was painted in late 1933, after he had been appointed an instructor at New York's Art Students League, a position he held for twenty years. Several objects in the still life function as symbols of the artist's prior employment before gaining the prestigious teaching position at the League.

The photograph of the *Portrait of Tadias Arias de Enriquez* by Francisco Goya (1746-1828), alludes to the artist's activity as a commercial photographer during the early 1920s, when he received commissions from galleries as well as from artist friends to photograph paintings and sculpture. The grapes and avocados symbolize the summers of 1907-1910 when Kuniyoshi worked seventeen to eighteen hour days picking fruit in Fresno and the Imperial Valley of California, so that he could earn enough money to attend the Los Angeles School of Art and Design during the winter. Kuniyoshi later related that grapes were included in his paintings as a symbolic reference to his "long hot summers picking them."[8]

Included in *Weathervane and Other Objects* is a sculpture mold by Kuniyoshi's friend Paul Fiene (1899-1949), and a folk art weathervane in the guise of a horse.[9] The mold is a symbol of formal art training, while the folk art sculpture represents an art unshackled by academic conventions. In his still life of 1933, Kuniyoshi makes reference to the primitive art that inspired his work of the early 1920s, when he developed appreciation for not only American folk art, but that of the Italian primitive Giotto (c.1266-1337), and Piero della Francesca (c.1420-1492). As Werner Haftmann noted, such art shared a "purely formal beauty . . . combined with a feeling for the pristine magical quality of the thing."[10]

In his art, Kuniyoshi consciously emulated the playful, romantic, and instinctive approach of the primitive artist, while retaining a modern outlook. In contrast to the animated horse in the Santa Barbara picture, Fiene's mold is turned upside down, suggesting the triumph of the unconstrained spirit of the folk artist. Meanwhile the disturbingly faceless portrait by the Spanish Romantic painter Goya "looks on" from the rear.

19. Yasuo Kuniyoshi, Watermelon, Fruit and Cigars, *1927, oil on canvas 25 × 30". Collection unknown.*

20. Yasuo Kuniyoshi, Photograph and Peaches on Chair, *1938, oil on canvas 49 × 39-1/4". Collection unknown.*

Kuniyoshi's embrace of the primitive and the contemporary is symbolized by the appearance of *Cahiers D'Art* in *Weathervane and Other Objects. Cahiers D'Art* was the outstanding avant garde art periodical of its day. The issue featured in the painting, number five-six, appeared in the Fall of 1933, and included lavishly illustrated articles on Hans Arp, Max Ernst and Juan Gris. In addition to publishing studies of French modernists, the magazine featured extensive articles on primitive art. In the same issue, a lengthy account appeared on Minoan painting and sculpture.

Other Kuniyoshi still lifes feature black and white photographic reproductions of paintings of young women by Titian (c.1490-1576), Peter Paul Rubens (1577-1640), and Henri Matisse (1869-1954).[11] With tongue in cheek, he plays off a photograph's two dimensional nature for dramatic and slightly comic effect. In *Watermelon, Fruits and Cigars* (il. 19), Goya's portrait is placed atop the arrangement upon a wall, while in *Still Life* (former collec-

tion of Jean Mauze), and *Photograph and Peaches on Chair* (il. 20), the Matisse and Rubens images act as the support for other objects. The appearance of the photographs also reflect Kuniyoshi's acknowledgement of artists he greatly admired, and their consummate treatment of women.

When not including photographs in his still life compositions, Kuniyoshi often substituted a newspaper or magazine cover or illustration. The publication was usually a tabloid, frequently the *New York Daily News* or the *Police Gazette.* The image of a young fashionably attired woman is generally discovered below a headline. One is almost never able to read the words which appear in Kuniyoshi's paintings, unlike that of the art of his close friend Reginald Marsh (1898-1954).

The introduction of illustrational material also served to allow Kuniyoshi to explore his interest in half-tones. He commented:

I believe most great paintings are controlled with half-

21. Yasuo Kuniyoshi, From the Boardwalk, *1936, lithograph, 9-1/4 × 12-5/16". Collection of the Museum of Modern Art. Given anonymously.*

tones. Here and there lights are brought out and darks are pushed back. Where the half-tones are one finds more color than in the darks or in the lights.

    Colors are important in a way but it isn't everything . . . you can create colors even in black and white. If you can translate the value of colors into black and white.[12]

In the photographs and other illustrational material that appear in his paintings, Kuniyoshi transposed his lithographic method of emphasizing semitints and tonal relations, subtleties of light and shade, occasionally applying smudges of tone for expressive effect (il. 21).[13]

    Kuniyoshi looked upon painting inanimate objects as a challenge. During the 1930s, he frequently sought to make them come alive and take on a presence that would

have been impossible were they treated individually. In 1944, he remarked:

    Still life is a difficult thing to paint. I find it more difficult to start than figure or landscape. You have to deal with . . . lifeless things. To make them alive is harder . . . But I've learned a great deal . . . from painting still life because you can work as hard as you want to and as long as you want and still keep the same position.[14]

Occasionally, Kuniyoshi figuratively brought inanimate objects to life, creating arrangements that suggest the human form. In *Artificial Flower* (il. 22), he painted what appears to be a petticoat immediately below a photograph of Titian's sensual and highly naturalistic painting *La Madellena.* Kuniyoshi's painting is a wry and ironic

22. *Yasuo Kuniyoshi,* Artificial Flower, *1934, lithograph, 9-1/4 × 10-1/4" (irregular). Collection of the Museum of Modern Art. Given anonymously.*

commentary on the nature of reality and illusion. Not only does he not paint an actual woman, but the rose is artificial, a manufactured floral design appears upon the scarf, and the flower upon the vase is hand painted. The playing card allowed him to include a black and white element as counterpoint to the photograph of the Titian painting. Perhaps Kuniyoshi also wanted the spade motif to be associated with the floral elements, as it resembles a heart with a stalk at the juncture of the lobes.[15]

In *Things on Iron Chair* (il. 23), objects are engaged in a metaphorical dialogue upon a seat, as in *Weathervane and Other Objects* (il. 18). Kuniyoshi cleverly placed them within a human context, as if posed for a group portrait. Rather than painting a woman, boxers, flowers, or watermelon and grapes from nature, he painted a vase bearing the inscription Juanita, a news-

paper or magazine photograph of a boxing match, a flowered scarf, and his own still life of fruit, resting on an ornate wrought iron chair. He included no living organisms, conveying the notion that art has the special capacity to give life to inanimate things, and that what you see in a painting is, after all, only an illusion.

23. *Yasuo Kuniyoshi,* Things on Iron Chair, *1936, oil on canvas, 44-1/4 × 34". Collection of The Whitney Museum of American Art. Given in Memory of Edith Gregor Halpert by the Halpert Fund.*

24. *Anonymous,* Boxing, *c. 1935, photograph.*

25. *Yasuo Kuniyoshi,* Accordion and Horse, *1938, oil on canvas, 38-1/8 × 48". Collection of The Metropolitan Museum of Art. The Edward Joseph Gallagher Memorial Collection, 1956.*

Kuniyoshi also sought to make his still lifes come alive by emphasizing textures. He skillfully built up thin and smooth surfaces and thick impasto, occasionally allowing the coarse linen support to also act as a texture. His highly activated backgrounds of curling lines, scratches, and cloudy shapes verge on abstraction, leading one writer to call them a "mussy halo of phosphorescence."[16]

Kuniyoshi desired that objects as well as the architectural setting and space be "felt" and express the "realization of facts."[17] He related the following advice to his students:

Paint according to what you feel . . . Like the cement floor—is it hard, cold, solid? Understand what it is all about and paint accordingly. A certain material—the body, soft and warm, a box, solid, hollow inside. A landscape. Don't paint an impression. If you don't understand it, go five miles and see it.[18]

Kuniyoshi's paintings are highly tactile. Paint is richly and sensually applied. As Jeannette Lowe remarked:

One wants to touch the rich brown boards of his floors or run one's fingers over the curve of a Victorian chair or the surface of a simple, crude wooden table . . . One is fascinated by a feeling of the actual, the tangible, and no sooner is this tactile sense ar-

rested than the artist carries [you] off into a world of color and form completely that of the imagination.[19]

In *Accordion and Horse* (il. 25), Kuniyoshi animated the objects and the interior space by contrasting the various textures, colors, and the comparative weight, mass, and expressive movement of each object. Atop the still life arrangement is a small somewhat worn, iron prancing horse painted bright yellow. A large bulky ochre and olive green accordion supports the horse as well as the brown basket and red silk scarf with its dark green floral design. The shopworn musical instrument rests upon a ruffled copy of the *New York Daily News* and Kuniyoshi's painting table. Upon the newspaper in the area below the headline is the face of a young woman.

An article on Kuniyoshi in *PM* featured a photograph of *Accordion and Horse* and the still life arrangement that he had set up in his studio (il. 26). The writer related:

Here's a striking example of how a fine artist can

26. *Yasuo Kuniyoshi,* Accordion and Horse and Studio Set-up, *1938, photograph, 7-1/2 × 9-1/2". Collection of Sara M. Kuniyoshi.*

make ordinary things come excitingly alive! Kuniyoshi has taken a simple arrangement of inanimate objects, as seen by the camera's eye at left. An iron horse, scarf, accordion, newspaper—nothing inspiring about that. But—compare the photographed grouping with the painting . . . By his subtle handling of paint, by his skillful arrangement of lights and darks, the artist endows the commonplace items with a beautiful and decorative quality which simply did not exist before he created it. Now you can almost see the horse prance.[20]

The most immediately recognizable difference between the painting and the photographic record of *Accordion and Horse* made by the staff photographer, is the angle of approach. Beginning with his student still lifes of 1917-1920, Kuniyoshi emulated the angle of inclination favored by Paul Cézanne (1839-1905) in his Post-Impressionist still lifes, adopting a view from above, so that the support appears to be tilted.[21] He also emulated the French artist's placement of relatively heavy objects upon cloths and other lightweight materials. This served to create the illusion that they were being kept from falling, even though their suspension, as well as that of other elements, apppears impossible. Sometimes this is the sole function of objects.

In *Lay Figure* (il. 27), Kuniyoshi imbued an artist's mannequin with life. He dressed the jointed model in what appears to be a sheer black nightgown, as well as placing a scarf around her face, which contains a white and black paisley-like design around its border. She is stretched out upon a weathered ochre wicker chair. Upon the painting's receiving second prize at the 1939 *Annual International Exhibition of Paintings* at the Carnegie Institute, art critics were quick to point out the figure's lifelike appearance and curious pose: "The artist's lay figure stretched across the unclear wreck of a chair, twisted, abandoned, and forgotten . . . is still haunted by febrile yearnings."[22] Jeanette Lowe felt that the artist was motivated by a "whimsical turn of mind . . . the lady hurled upon a crazy chair in an improbable attitude, is surrounded by reading matter of which she had apparently wearied."[23]

Lay Figure was painted in 1938, after Kuniyoshi had begun a series of landscapes of ghost towns (il. 27). He now began to imbue his subjects with a haunted mood of desolation, perhaps motivated by the Great Depression and the prevailing Social Realist style of American art. In later years he often described himself as a sad and lonely man, explaining that this led him to paint "sorrowful things."[24]

Kuniyoshi was very fond of the wicker chair appearing in *Lay Figure*, and included it in a number of his pictures, as well as in one photograph. *Old Chair* (il. 28), is a study in textures and the play of light and shadow. Another photograph (il. 9) includes the mannequin as well as the artist Morris Kantor (1896-1974).

Beginning in 1940, Kuniyoshi's art was irrevocably affected and shaped by world events. In his still lifes he continued to utilize photographs and other illustrational material, folk art objects, vases, pitchers, scarves, and sculpture, and reintroduced ideas and motifs originally appearing in drawings and paintings from the 1920s, as well

27. Yasuo Kuniyoshi, Lay Figure, *1938, oil on canvas, 38-1/8 × 58-1/4". Collection Walker Art Center.*

28. Yasuo Kuniyoshi, Old Chair, *c. 1935-1939, photograph, 8 × 10". Collection of Sara M. Kuniyoshi.*

as reshuffling more recent compositions.

In his still lifes of the early 1940s, Kuniyoshi's underlying theme was the ephemerality and transitoriness of life. He treated objects as lifeless ruins, as victims of time or violence. These paintings reflect his feelings of hopelessness, that everything around him seemed "broken, worn, used up . . . rotting."[25]

Kuniyoshi's pictorial world became one of chaos and agitation. He became increasingly morbid and cynical. In the posters and drawings he created under the auspices of the Office of War Information, he graphically recorded the cruelty of man at war, emulating Goya's *Disasters of War*. His art became increasingly dramatic and somber, and his treatment of form, chiaroscuro and space ever more exaggerated.

Inspired by the traditional still life subject of memento mori, Kuniyoshi evoked the precariousness of man's existence and time's inexorable sway over life and matter. He placed broken, decaying, and torn objects in disorderly ar-

29. *Yasuo Kuniyoshi,* Upside Down Table and Mask, *1940, oil on canvas, 60-1/8 × 30-1/2". Collection of The Museum of Modern Art. Acquired through the Lillie Bliss Bequest.*

rangements, strewn over table tops or in strange and mysterious settings. Kuniyoshi related his reasoning in 1944:

> If a man feels very deeply about the war, or any sorrow or gladness, his feeling should be symbolized in his expression, no matter what medium he chooses. Let us say still life. Still life is out of mode right now, but you can use symbols to say clearly how the sorrow or gladness is felt deeply in your heart, although

30. *Yasuo Kuniyoshi,* I Think So, *1938, oil on canvas 40 × 31". Albright-Knox Gallery. Room of Contemporary Art Fund, 1939.*

> the physical expression of it is just still life . . . one can get the feelings of the man from looking at it.[26]

In *Upside Down Table and Mask* (il. 29), Kuniyoshi sought to express his feelings about the war raging abroad.[27] The broken table is precariously balanced upon another table, covered by a white cloth. The newspaper, blue vase, and fragment of gold tassel appear to be on the verge of falling off the tilted support. The cord around the vase is broken, perhaps having snapped under strain. The folding ruler hanging from the base of the overturned table is bent out of shape.

The painting brings several of Kuniyoshi's pictorial ideas together in a new way. The mask and scarf in conjunction with the broken base of the table suggest the shape of a human figure, recalling *Artificial Flower* (il. 22). The Museum of Modern Art painting exudes the overt theatricality of *Lay Figure* (il. 27); a clown mask has been substituted for a mannequin. On the table's underside is a copy of the *New York Daily News* with an unreadable headline and picture of a fashionably attired young woman. Like the models in many of his figurative

31. *Yasuo Kuniyoshi,* End of Juanita, *oil on canvas,*
34 × 44". Collection of Edith and Milton Lowenthal, New York.

32. *Yasuo Kuniyoshi,* Model, Back, *1937, photograph.*
Collection of Sara M. Kuniyoshi.

33. *Yasuo Kuniyoshi,* Standing Nude, *c. 1939-1941,*
Maroger medium, 16 × 12". Collection of Paul Jenkins.

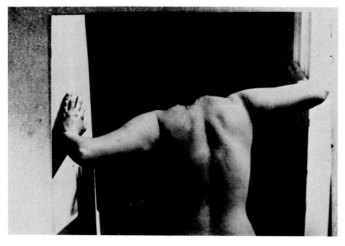

paintings of the 1930s (il. 30), she is calm and reflective,
an image of contemplation amidst frenzy.

    End of Juanita (il. 31), was painted in 1942. Ob-

jects in *Things on Iron Chair* (il. 23), reappear; the same
pitcher, now without an inscription, and the artist's painting of a watermelon and grapes. The still life pictured
within this painting ironically serves as a support for objects, as reproductions of paintings by Rubens and
Matisse had in two of his works of the 1930s. Peaches,
black cloth, a box of matches, and a photograph rest
upon the fruit still life. The photograph closely resembles
Kuniyoshi's own picture of a nude woman viewed from
the back with her arms raised (il. 32).

    Whereas Kuniyoshi had sought to symbolically
bring Juanita to life in *Things on Iron Chair,* now he
represents her demise. Though she is not broken,
Juanita is partially wrapped and draped in a black cloth,
an allusion to death. With a touch of humour, Kuniyoshi
placed the nude posterior of the model beside the pitcher. He even seems to have added this portion of the
woman's body to the original photograph to be able to do

34. Yasuo Kuniyoshi, Broken Objects, *1944, oil on canvas,*
30 × 50-1/4". Collection of Metropolitan Museum of Art,
Gift of Mr. and Mrs. Allan D. Emil. 1963.

so. Atop the arrangement is a bird, which Kuniyoshi occasionally placed in close proximity to women in his
paintings. In his 1932 mural for the Women's Powder
Room of the Radio City Music Hall, a single bird appears
above the one entrance and exit door, on the inside of
the room.

The table and objects in *End of Juanita* are placed in
a murky and mysterious outdoor setting, conveying a
mood of emptiness and desolation. The landscape is
ochre and grey, and contains the swirling shapes discovered on the background wall of many of his still life
and figurative paintings. Kuniyoshi's trip to the
Southwest in 1941 inspired him to paint the "essence of
those places." He had been impressed by its "vastness
and primitiveness." He felt it had the appearance of the
"beginning of creation," and found the mountains "very
volcanic."[28] Upon his return to New York, he began to include a volcanic-like mountain shape regularly in his
works. It can be seen to the right of center in *End of
Juanita.*

In addition to landscape, Kuniyoshi introduced a
nude into his still life. Like the partially (il. 33) and fully
unclad women of his figurative paintings, she has broad
hips, powerful buttocks, and heavy arms. The physical
type brings to mind the sculpture of Gaston Lachaise
(1882-1935).

In an interview with Lloyd Goodrich, Kuniyoshi
remarked that the world situation motivated him to
"create still lifes [that] were more than still lifes . . . people sometimes say of an artist that he is nothing but a still
life painter, but . . . you can paint any subject — still life,
nudes, landscape — and get all kinds of implications into
it." He also noted that in his own still lifes "there were all
kinds of elements that suggest things ouside of still
life."[29]

In 1944, Kuniyoshi wrote cryptic notes expressing
consternation over still life's role in contemporary art,
comparing it to the past when it was not considered of
any importance within the hierarchy of art:

Still life was never fashionable or artist felt it was
important. There was always still life painter, painted

35. *Yasuo Kuniyoshi,* Japanese Toy Tiger and Other Objects, *1932, oil on canvas, 34 × 49-1/2". Collection unknown.*

[for] Old Master, if flower necessary in picture. Until time of Chardin [there were] very little still lifes [painted] . . . since nothing much happened till Cézanne's time. Renoir and he painted great still lifes and I was very much aware in my student days that still lifes could be just as important and I painted a great many still lifes myself.

Somehow still lifes today are not as fashionable or people don't give much thought to it as even in my student days. Today they make little pretty things for mantlepiece or pretty flowers to decorate the dining room.

I haven't [really] seen still life . . . tackled with same enthusiasm or trying to solve certain problems. I've found none of these exist today.

I maintain always that my attitude toward still life is [that it is] something we all paint and I stress that attitude to my students whenever I have chance because I learned a great deal from painting still life.[30]

After the surprise attack on Pearl Harbor, the Japanese-born Kuniyoshi was interned in his Fourteenth Street studio in Manhattan.[31] Two days later he reported to a New York police station to surrender his camera and a pair of binoculars. With the support of his many friends in the art world, Kuniyoshi was permitted to lead a relatively normal life during the war years. He volunteered his services to the Office of War Information, making two speeches against Japan, which were broadcast over short wave radio in early 1942, and designed war posters and drawings illustrating enemy acts of torture and cruelty. The immigration law which would have allowed him to gain the American citizenship he had long desired only went into effect shortly before his death in 1953.

Broken Objects (il. 34) was executed in 1944. One glass appears upon the painting table, while another has fallen on the pitcher Juanita, shattering her handle. A photograph closely resembling one of his own is torn in two (fig. 14). Among the objects included is a red cloth, what appears to be a grey-green ribbon, and a fragment of the cover of a brown and white cigar box, upon which is written the brand name Optima.

As in *End of Juanita*, objects do not lie directly upon a wooden table. Here they are placed upon a transparent piece of white cotton or silk, perhaps a scarf. As in other still lifes of the early 1940s, objects appear larger than in earlier works because they have been brought closer to the picture plane, while the base of the table has been abruptly cut off by the bottom edge of the canvas.

A possible clue to the meaning of *Broken Objects*, may lie in a painting of twelve years earlier, entitled *Japanese Toy Tiger and Odd Objects* (il. 35). Executed upon the artist's return from a visit to his native Japan, the picture contains a similar choice of objects and arrangement around a pitcher. As in *Broken Objects*, the support is Kuniyoshi's painting table. Upon it is his pair of binoculars, which would be taken from him after Japan's attack on Pearl Harbor. Cigars appear, as does a cord and tassel. The toy paper-mâché tiger was one of a pair the artist purchased in Japan. *Japanese Toy Tiger and Odd Objects* was painted at the end of a five year period when Kuniyoshi was including exotic objects in some of his still lifes, before imbuing them with an overt symbolic content.

In *Broken Objects,* the torn photograph takes the place of the binoculars on the table. In destroying the photograph of the nude woman, Kuniyoshi symbolically alluded to what the government had done to his career as a photographer. In his two speeches for the Office of War Information, he sought above all to reach Japanese artists, writers, musicians and others interested in culture. He outlined the major successes of his life in order to illustrate the benefits of democracy as opposed to a militarist and totalitarian society, and the ease and freedom with which he was presently living as an artist in the United States.[32] Such propagandistic pronouncements avoided the issue of what the government had done with his camera, as well as his own compassionate feeling that the Japanese internment camps in the Western United States were anti-democratic.[33]

In October, 1944, Kuniyoshi's *Room 110* (il. 36), was awarded first prize at the Carnegie Institute exhibition *Painting in the United States.* The choice inspired several sarcastic articles in the Pittsburgh press, stimulated by his

status as an enemy alien, a reluctance to seriously accept the value of Kuniyoshi's selection and combination of elements, as well as his impossibly tilted table top still life.[34] Perhaps motivated by the storm of controversy, Kuniyoshi shortly thereafter commented on the painting in his autobiographical notes:

> I have assiduously collected throughout the years numerous objects of various shapes, textures and colors because of their special appeal to me, and with the thought of using them in my painting. My approach to these objects, for painting purposes, is from the psychological as well as the emotional viewpoint, setting them in a relationship and environment that creates an association stemming from personal experience. Room 110 *has no story. If there is a story it is one of complexities, dealing with elimination and destruction, pictorially re-created as a reflection of my life.*[35]

The title of the painting and the inclusion of the number 110 in reverse in the background, as it would appear on a door viewed from the interior, is an explicit reference to 110 Columbia Heights in Brooklyn. Kuniyoshi's patron Hamilton Easter Field (1873-1922), provided him and his first wife Katherine Schmidt a one room apartment rent free in this building from 1919 through early 1922. Upon Field's death the sculptor Robert Laurent (1890-1970) furnished the Kuniyoshis with a basement apartment next door at Field's former home. The couple remained there until 1931, when they settled independently in Manhattan.[36]

In *Room 110*, like *Weathervane and Other Objects* (il. 18), Kuniyoshi alluded to his earlier life. Once more a cluster of grapes appears. It was during his first several years in Brooklyn that he worked as a commercial photographer, as well as a framemaker and art instructor, while hoping to establish his reputation so that he would be able to give more time to his art. As Doreen A. Bolger related, the Field environment was the focal point for "a group of young, struggling artists who were attracted by his personality and the assistance he offered them."[37]

The composition, placement of the umbrella, as well as the inclusion of the grapes, indicate that Kuniyoshi modeled *Room 110* upon his 1928 painting *Alabaster Vase and Fruit* (il. 37). Perhaps he was motivated to utilize that still life because it was in a Brooklyn collection, having been given to the Brooklyn Museum in 1938. The painting is representative of Kuniyoshi's style of the late 1920s, before be sought to revitalize his still lifes with imagination and symbolism.

In *Room 110*, Kuniyoshi updated his earlier picture,

36. Yasuo Kuniyoshi, Room 110, 1944, oil on canvas, 44 × 34".
F.M. Hall Collection, Sheldon Memorial Gallery, University of Nebraska.

37. *Yasuo Kuniyoshi*, Alabaster Vase and Fruit, *1928,
oil on canvas, Brooklyn Museum of Art; Gift of Sam A. Lewisohn.*

38. *Yasuo Kuniyoshi*, Rotting on the Shore, *1945, oil on canvas,
46-1/8 × 36-1/8". Collection of Norton Gallery and School of Art.*

including symbolic references, bringing objects up even closer to the picture plane, severely cropping the base of the table, introducing his lighter more vibrant palette, and animating the surface with his almost calligraphic use of line. At the same time he also "borrowed" from the 1928 painting, placing objects one atop the other, overlapping shapes, emphasizing the flatness of each form and the two dimensional nature of the picture plane.

In *Room 110*, Kuniyoshi included objects which he featured in his still lifes of a decade or more before. The broken blue vase, hanging from a string, was included unscathed in *Odd Objects on a Couch* (1930, Collection of the Philadelpha Museum of Art). Draped around the umbrella handle is a rose with a stem and leaf. Kuniyoshi rarely painted flowers after completing his 1932 mural for the Women's Powder Room of the Radio City Music Hall in New York, in which flower blossoms and fronds of foliage appear larger than life in a landscape setting. Afterward Kuniyoshi chose instead to regularly include scarves with

floral designs. Additionally, in his still lifes of 1927 and 1928 he almost always chose to include a leaf or a stem.

Room 110 also reflects Kuniyoshi's desire in the early 1940s to extend the traditional notion of the still life. The interior takes on the ambience of a genre scene; the use of the semi-transparent glass allowed him to express the effect of light filtering through it from the other side. The magazine illustration of a woman in a bathing suit recalls Kuniyoshi's treatment of swimmers and people at the beach of earlier years, while also serving to intimate the notion of figure painting within the matrix of a still life, just as the photographs in *End of Juanita* and *Broken Objects* referred to the subject of the nude.

Atop the still life is a ragged and deteriorating object draped by a cloth, upon which appears a letter or monogram. The object is difficult to identify. A Pittsburgh newspaper reporter suggested that it was "a torn piece of cardboard, a fragment of metal, or a wet rag hung out to dry."[38] Regardless, the article, like the cracked blue vase,

39. Yasuo Kuniyoshi, Fisherman's Son, *1922, oil on canvas, 20 × 24". Collection unknown.*

is deteriorating, reflecting Kuniyoshi's opinion of the state of the world during World War II. *Room 110* also conveys Kuniyoshi's own feeling at the time about his past. In August, 1944, when he may have been completing the picture, he wrote:

> As I grow older I see things in a more severe way . . . than I used to . . . . I used to think life was glorious and always sunny. It isn't that I enjoy beginning to feel that way about it but somehow the things I remember in the past are not joy or happiness but things I suffered which I remember far better, and to-day I am confronted with that kind of tendency, not because I'm inviting it but problems seem to pile up one thing on top of another and perhaps my life may be built on this basis. So that I have to accept it and make use of it to my advantage as well as I can. Years ago people called me a cynic but I didn't really know what that meant or really didn't think I was then, but today I am indeed more inclined toward that direction. I think what I'm doing today, if I can generalize, is a cynical attitude towards world in general. . . . it appears to be on the surface of my paintings. . . . I try to . . . state that as clearly as I can.[39]

Rotting on the Shore (il. 38), in the collection of the Norton Gallery of Art, was begun in the summer of 1944 and completed in the winter of 1945, in time to be exhibited at Kuniyoshi's first one-man showing at The Downtown Gallery in seven years.[40] The artist later remarked that the painting was "something like early drawings but much more mature," and that he was trying to create a "simpler" statement than in the past but with "deeper expression."[41] In addition to reintroducing elements of his early style, Kuniyoshi expanded upon particular motifs and subjects of the past.

From 1918 through 1924, Kuniyoshi spent summers in Ogunquit, Maine, where Field operated the Ogunquit School of Painting and Sculpture. Kuniyoshi, like Marsden Hartley (1877-1943), Bernard Karfiol (1886-1952), Stefan Hirsh (1899-1964), and other artists, lived in one of the fishing shacks lining Perkins Cove. He quickly made friends with the fishermen, and executed many paintings and drawings featuring them and their children (il. 39), as well as menacing octopuses seeking to devour their catch (il. 40).[42]

In *Rotting on the Shore* Kuniyoshi sought to create a simpler, more direct statement than in his recent still lifes, and turned to the past for help. His treatment of the fish recalls early ink drawings such as *Octopus,* in which he favored placing a form at or near the center of the com-

40. *Yasuo Kuniyoshi,* Octopus, *1922, ink on paper, 15-3/4 × 10-1/4". Collection unknown.*

position, so that it appears to hover above the ground. The peculiar emergence of the tree branch suggests comparison with his treatment of spiky plants in his drawings, which seem to rise portentiously from the earth. As in his painting *Fisherman's Son* (il. 39), Kuniyoshi employed bird's-eye perspective, and stressed distortion of scale and spatial dislocation. He placed elements one atop the other, utilizing outline to define forms, placing them in asymmetrical arrangements, all pictorial devices which initially evolved from his study of American folk painting and the art of Paul Cézanne.

41. *Yasuo Kuniyoshi,* Pears, Grapes and Peaches, *1927, transfer lithograph printed in black, 16-1/16 × 12-1/8. Collection of the Museum of Modern Art. Given anonymously.*

As in his art of 1920-1926, Kuniyoshi utilized his memory to paint elements, desiring to add "much more of [the] things he [felt] should be emphasized."[43] He was "sort of juggling things around."[44] His landscape, for example, was executed from memory of the environment of Provinceton, Massachusetts, which he visited often. He repeated "certain spots that he found interesting . . . drawing a sort of composite."[45]

Despite Kuniyoshi's readoption of earlier practices, *Rotting on the Shore* was painted in a style reflective of his more recent art, and the picture retains a strong feeling of the real world. He now sought to combine "the idea and the reality, to paint ideas as in his early work with the feeling of reality of his middle work."[46] This reality is mystifying and symbolic.

Kuniyoshi's handling of paint is sensual and rich. Through the application of cool and warm colors, forms appear to push forward as well as recede in space. His palette seems more Cézannesque than usual, including an equal emphasis on shades of green, red, blue-grey, brown and yellow. Kuniyoshi emphasized textures more selectively than in many of the works previously discussed, accentuating only those forms which appear to push forward, such as the mounted fish, the fruit bowl, the three rocks, and the cloud forms in the sky. The surface of the blue-grey inner wall is lightly painted, and he allowed the canvas to show through at top left.

Again Kuniyoshi used objects as weights; one rock attempts to keep the bowl stationary, while another rests upon a lightweight and transparent piece of material serving to keep it from blowing away, and a third supports a wedge which helps keep a wood board propped up against the mounted fish. The landscape appears to tilt downward, creating the illusion that the objects are suspended or floating in space, despite the various encumbrances.

In *Rotting on the Shore* Kuniyoshi continued to extend the boundaries of still life painting. He reversed the normal interior/exterior relationship of his still lifes of the late 1920s, which feature an arrangement of objects upon a table with a view out the window into a landscape (il. 38). While evoking the tradition of the game or sporting still life, Kuniyoshi also throws a curve, presenting the prized catch as a decaying salmon. *Rotting on the Shore* can be considered partly a landscape, partly an interior view, and partly a game still life in a broken fruit bowl.

The bare tree branch rising from bottom right of center, at the point where the window ends and the landscape begins, is an enlargement of a motif that appears frequently in Kuniyoshi's paintings, drawings, and lithographs of 1921-1928, in compositions featuring an interior and view. In such examples the branch was placed similarly, or in the landscape (il. 41), and was barely noticeable. As the artist reversed the relationship, the form is made immensely larger.

The bare tree branch in his early genre paintings (il. 42) and relatively straightforward still life compositions of the 1920s acts almost as a remarque, as a sign of the artist's moral presence. In *Boy Stealing Fruit*, the imminent theft of a banana and apples is heightened by the inclusion of a view of a church steeple through the window at top left, with the branch peeking up just outside.

Kuniyoshi evidently felt some psychic identity with the tree, as well as with the fish. For the dust jacket of the catalogue of his 1948 Whitney Museum of American Art retrospective exhibition he executed an original drawing of a fish lying upon a bowl, placing it just above his name. Perhaps Kuniyoshi's infatuation evolved out of his study of primitive art or his upbringing as a Buddhist. As Carl G. Jung related:

> Among . . . [primitive people] whose consciousness is at a far different level from ours, the "soul" (or psyche) is not felt to be a unit. Many primitives assume that a man has a "bush soul" as well as his own, and that this bush soul is incarnate in a wild animal or a tree, with which the human individual has some kind of psychic identity. This is what the French ethnologist Lucien Levy-Bruhl called a "mystical participation" . . . It is a well known psychological fact that an individual may have such an unconscious identity with some other person or object.[47]

In Buddhism, everything, whether an animal, a mountain, or a tree, has a kami, or a soul, a spirit and a deity. Nature was inhabited by kami. In the Buddhist doctrine basic principles also accord that "no sooner has an individual arisen than disease and decay begin to act upon it," that "life was an unending succession of afflictions," and that "even form and other material qualities in things we find are impermanent and perishing."[48] At the moment of his death, Buddha exhorted that "Decay is inherent in all component things. Work out your salvation with silence."[49]

After 1941, Kuniyoshi's art regularly reflected a deep commitment to a humanistic point of view, symbolized in the art world by his activity as a founder and president of the Artists Equity Association. He became an outspoken advocate of various causes. He felt that "good art . . . must stem from humanity and contribute a spiritual concept."[50]

In *Rotting on the Shore*, a red cloth is draped over the

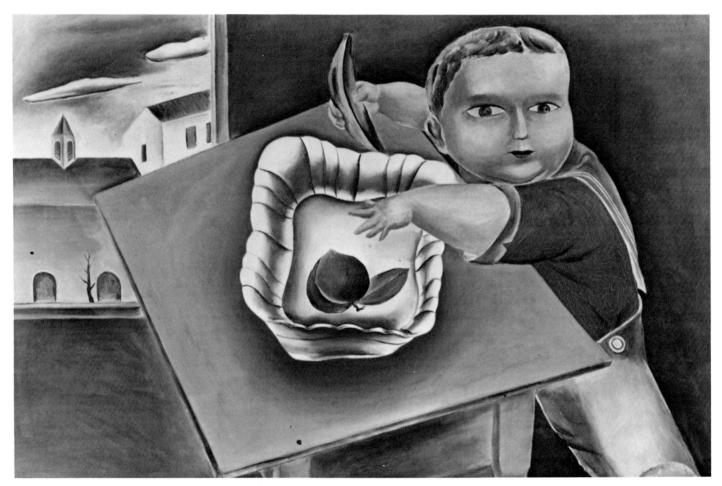

42. Yasuo Kuniyoshi, Boy Stealing Fruit, *1923,*
oil on canvas, 20 × 30". Columbus Museum of Art, Ohio;
Gift of Ferdinand Howard.

top of the mounted fish, recalling Kuniyoshi's use of a similar shroud-like covering in *End of Juanita* (il. 31), *Broken Objects* (il. 34), and *Room 110* (il. 36). Normally it would serve to cover the decaying fish from human sight, but now the drape has been lifted. The mount is also red, suggesting the color of blood. Sabura Miyamoto noted in analyzing Kuniyopshi's still lifes of the early 1940s, that "a thing can be painted as a vessel of human nature in the sense that it is a pitiless objective being to which insatiable human egoism has shaped itself."[51]

Kuniyoshi's belief that the world would never be the same with the coming of World War II, led him to drain the life and vitality from objects and subjects for which he had formerly expressed enthusiasm. During the summer of 1944, he wrote:

> *Morbidness has helped to shape and lead to feeling of depression. Afraid [of] myself. Such a feeling is perversion to see [and to] feel only a warped darker side of life. I believe and know clearly in my case such an attitude came entirely from suspense, frustration, all to do with myself creating morbid imagination.[52]*

In *Rotting on the Shore,* man's spiritual and physical relationship with nature no longer works. Now man is eliminated. All that is left are the spoils and ruins that he has left behind, and the "lower" life forms not affected by man's folly.

After the end of World War II, Kuniyoshi began to study Zen Buddhism. On more than one occasion, he expressed his philosophy of life and art by repeating the following passage written by Alan Watts in *The Spirit of Zen:*

> *Walk on! For we can only understand life by keeping pace with it, by a complete affirmation and acceptance of its magic-like transformations and unending changes . . . for everything is perpetually becoming new . . . for all things are at this moment passing away.[53]*

FOOTNOTES

1. Lloyd Goodrich, *Yasuo Kuniyoshi* (New York: Whitney Museum of American Art, 1948): 31-32.

2. In the summer of 1944, Kuniyoshi began to write an autobiography, dating each day's remarks. His discussion of still life painting occurred on November 18, 1944. This unpublished material is in the possession of Sara Kuniyoshi, and will hereafter be referred to as "Autobiographical Remarks."

3. No. 30 Kuniyoshi, unidentified museum handout, possession of Sara Kuniyoshi.

4. Lloyd Goodrich, "Notes on Conversation with Yasuo Kuniyoshi," Whitney Museum Papers, Archives of American Art, microfilm roll M670:84.

5. "Autobiographical Remarks," dated August 23, 1944.

6. Mary Meixner, "Kuniyoshi Talks to Students," *College Art Journal* 13 (Fall 1950): 12.

7. "Yasuo Kuniyoshi Exhibition Material," Whitney Museum Papers, Archives of American Art, microfilm roll N668:450A.

8. "Universality in Art," typescript of a lecture delivered by Yasuo Kuniyoshi, undated, possession of Sara Kuniyoshi.

9. Sara Kuniyoshi related in a conversation of May 20, 1983, that her husband had borrowed the sculpture mold from Fiene. Kuniyoshi referred to two of the elements in *Weathervane and Other Objects* in an interview for an article about his career at the time of his retrospective exhibition at the Whitney Museum of American Art in 1948:

> *I picked up all kinds of materials—cigars and toys and weathervanes and the old sofa in Woodstock, where I was going then. I picked them up for shapes, colors, textures—but . . . when they were all together they take on symbolism for me.*

Aline B. Louchheim, "Kuniyoshi: Look, My Past," *Art News* 47 (April 1948): 47.

10. Werner Haftmann, *Painting in the Twentieth Century* (New York: Frederick A. Praeger, Inc., Publications, 1969), p. 167.

11. See Franklin Riehlman and Tom Wolf, this catalog, p. 9.

12. "Autobiographical Remarks," dated August 26, 1944." Kuniyoshi also wrote:

> *For me, color does not mean very much. I used to paint with a lot of colors, partly because I was taught in the impressionist school, whose theory is to analyse colors within the small area. But later I found that unsatisfactory for the strong expression of feeling. I have been exercising with simpler colors. Although I use twelve colors, I try to create one color against another, and to create another color between those two . . . For instance, if I am painting a white towel I paint white all the way through first, and try to introduce cooler white and warmer white (that creates two colors right there) then light half-tones and darks within the white, so that this white towel is three tones and two colors. I treat other colors on other materials or objects the same way, so with five colors altogether in my painting there is much variety of tone and colors between one another.*

"Autobiographical Remarks," dated November 18, 1944.

13. Obviously in his photography Kuniyoshi was also involved with half-tones. At least on one occasion, he is known to have utilized a photograph as the model for a lithograph. See Franklin Riehlman and Tom Wolf, this catalog, p. 10.

14. "Autobiographical Remarks," dated August 24, 1944.

15. Sara Kuniyoshi relates not "artificial flower" was an expression applied by Kuniyoshi to women he found attractive. Conversation with Sara Kuniyoshi, May 20, 1983.

16. "Party," *Time Magazine,* February 6, 1939.

17. Yasuo Kuniyoshi, *Yasuo Kuniyoshi* (New York: American Artists Group, Inc., 1945), n.p.

18. Meixner, p. 12.

19. Jeannette Lowe, "Kuniyoshi Revisited: The Fertile Fantasy of a Mature Artist Seen Again," *Art News* 37 (January 28, 1939): 20.

20. "Yasuo Kuniyoshi," *PM,* January 18, 1944. Kuniyoshi hired a photographer to make a record of the appearance of *Headless Horse who Wants to Jump* (Collection of the Ohara Museum, Tokyo, Japan). The photograph is in the possession of Sara Kuniyoshi. This still life of 1945, and *Abandoned Treasures of 1946* (Collection of The High Museum of Art, Atlanta, Georgia), will not be discussed in this essay. Many of the ideas expressed here are applicable to those two paintings. Kuniyoshi also did a series of photographs of two different still life set-ups upon a table, whose very formal and relatively straightforward character imply that they may have been used for one of the artist's classes. (See illustration 26).

21. A recent exhibition at the Salander-O'Reilly Galleries in New York featured many of the artist's student still lifes, most of which were illustrated in the catalogue. See *Yasuo Kuniyoshi Paintings* (New York: Salander-O'Reilly Galleries, 1981).

22. "Kuniyoshi Wins Second," *Cleveland Plan Dealer,* October 22, 1939.

23. Lowe, p.8.

24. Meixner, p.11.

25. Louchheim, p.55.

26. "Autobiographical Remarks," dated November 8, 1944.

27. Conversation with Sara Kuniyoshi, May 20, 1983.

28. Kuniyoshi's remarks about the Southwest appear in "Autobiographical Remarks," dated August 26, 1944.

29. Goodrich, "Notes on Conversation with Yasuo Kuniyoshi," Whitney Museum Papers, Archives of American Art, microfilm roll M670: 85.

30. "Autobiographical Remarks," dated August 24, 1944.

31. Conversation with Sara Kuniyoshi, May 20, 1983.

32. English transcripts of Kuniyoshi's two speeches may be found in the Whitney Museum Papers, Archives of American Art, microfilm roll N669: 433-445.

33. For Kuniyoshi's opinion of the Japanese internment camps see "An Accumulation of Sadness," *PM,* November 27, 1944. Circumstantial evidence inspires speculation that *End of Juanita* and *Broken Objects* also reflect events transpiring in the artist's marital and extra-marital life, and that they symbolize the end of romantic relationships. In 1941, Kuniyoshi separated from his wife Sara and began a four year liaison with another woman. Their relationship ended in early 1944, the year he painted *Broken Objects.* Juanita was purchased by Sara and Yasuo Kuniyoshi on their honeymoon in Mexico in 1935. They both shared a great fondness for the pitcher and the memories it recalled. Sara Kuniyoshi recalls her husband informing her after their reconciliation in late 1945, that the pitcher had broken during their separation. One may conjecture that *End of Juanita* alludes to the break-up of his marriage, while *Broken Objects* refers to his two failed relationships of the early 1940s. One question remains unanswered: could the model who appears in the photograph in both paintings be the other woman in Kuniyoshi's life? Information regarding Juanita was related by Sara Kuniyoshi in a conversation of May 20, 1983.

34. See for example, "Study in Contrasts," *The Pittsburgh Press,* October 29, 1944.

35. "Autobiographical Remarks," dated December 29, 1944.

36. Robert Laurent, "Memories of Yas," *College Art Journal* 13 (Fall 1953): 8.

37. Doreen A. Bolger, "Hamilton Easter Field and the Rise of Modern Art in America," unpublished M.A. thesis, University of Delaware, p. 63.

38. Douglas Naylor, "Maybe It's Symbol—Art Jury Given 1st to Japanese's Painting: Winner Depicts 'Pile of Junk,' " *The Pittsburgh Press,* October 13, 1946.

39. "Autobiographical Remarks," dated August 21, 1944.

40. Goodrich, "Notes on Conversation with Yasuo Kuniyoshi," Whitney Museum Papers, Archives of American Art, microfilm roll M670: 62.

41. Ibid., microfilm roll M670: 70.

42. For an account of some of Kuniyoshi's experiences with the Maine fishermen see Robert Laurent, "Memories of Yas," pp. 7-8.

43. Goodrich, "Notes on Conversation with Yasuo Kuniyoshi," Whitney Museum Papers, Archives of American Art, Microfilm roll M670: 70.

44. Ibid.

45. Ibid., microfilm roll M670: 73.

46. Ibid., microfilm roll M670: 62.

47. Carl G. Jung, editor and introduction, *Man and his Symbols* (New York: Dell Publishing Company, 1969), pp. 6-7. When questioned why a cow appeared so frequently in his art of the early 1920's, Kuniyoshi remarked: "I felt very near to the cow. Besides I thought I understood the animal. You see I was born, judging by the Japanese calendar, in a 'cow year.' According to the legend I believed my fate to be guided, more or less, by the bovine kingdom." Yasuo Kuniyoshi, "East to West," *Magazine of Art* 33 (February 1940): 75, 77.

48. Heinrich Dumoulin, editor, John C. Maraldo, associative editor, *Buddhism in the Modern World* (New York: Macmillan Publishing Co., Inc., 1976), p. 6.

49. Ibid., p. 7.

50. "Kuniyoshi Gets Record Crowd at Art Center," *Clearwater Sun,* February 28, 1952.

51. Saburo Miyamoto, "Forgotten Time and Space," *Mainichi,* March 18,1954. English translation in possession of Sara Kuniyoshi.

52. "Autobiographical Remarks," dated August 22, 1944.

53. Alan Wilson Watts, *The Spirit of Zen* (London: J. Murray, 1936), p. 135.

EXHIBITION CHECKLIST YASUO KUNIYOSHI

*PHOTOGRAPHS

Mexico, 1935
10-11/16 × 7-9/16" (24.5 × 19.3 cm)
Water Lily, 1936
8 × 10" (20.3 × 25.2 cm)
From the Boardwalk, 1936
7-3/8 × 9-3/8" (18.8 × 24 cm)
Nude, 1936
8 × 10" (20.3 × 25.3 cm)
42nd Street Ferry, 1937
5½ × 9½" (14.2 × 24.1 cm)
Head of Model #1, 1937
7 × 9½" (17.7 × 24.2 cm)
Head of Model #2, 1937
7½ × 9½" (19 × 24.2 cm)
Arnold Blanche, 1937
7½ × 9½" (19.3 × 24.2 cm)
Elsie Speicher, 1937
7½ × 9½" (19.2 × 24.2 cm)
Collection Andrée Ruellan
Rosella Hartman Swimming, 1937
8 × 10" (20.2 × 25.2 cm)
Model, 1937
9½ × 7½" (24.2 × 19.2 cm)
Torso, 1937
9½ × 7½" (24.3 × 19.1 cm)
May Day Parade, 1937
7½ × 9½" (19.1 × 24.3 cm)
Abandoned Woodshed, 1937
7-5/16 × 9½" (18.6 × 24.3 cm)
Abandoned Woodshed Texture, 1937
7-5/8 × 9½" (19.4 × 24.3 cm)
Boy Diving, Coney Island, 1938
7-5/8 × 9-5/8" (19 × 24.3 cm)
Boy Sketching, Spectators, Coney Island,
1938 7½ × 9½" (19.5 × 24.4 cm)
Sketch Class, Coney Island, 1938
7¼ × 9¼" (18.7 × 23.9 cm)
Bicyclists, World's Fair Parade, 1938
7-5/8 × 9-5/8" (19.5 × 24.4 cm)
Crowd, World's Fair Parade, 1938
7½ × 9½" (19.3 × 24.3 cm)
Welcome to New York, 1938
7-1/8 × 9-5/8" (18.1 × 24.4 cm)
Union Square, 1938
7-1/8 × 9-9/16" (18.1 × 24.3 cm)
Women on Shore, 1938
7½ × 9-9/16" (19 × 24.3 cm)
Swimmer and Rowboat, 1938
7-9/16 × 9-5/8" (19.3 × 24.4 cm)
Class Picnic, 1938
7½ × 9-7/16" (19 × 24 cm)
Crane, East Kingston, 1938
7½ × 9½" (19 × 24 cm)
*Abandoned Farm Machinery,
East Kingston*, 1938
7-9/16 × 9-3/8" (19.3 × 23.9 cm)
Drill, East Kingston, 1938
7-5/8 × 9-9/16" (19.5 × 24.3 cm)
Seagulls, Rockport, Mass, 1938
7-9/16 × 9-5/8" (19.3 × 24.4 cm)
Man and Mast, Rockport, Mass., 1938
9-9/16 × 7-3/8" (24.3 × 18.7 cm)

Wall and Traps, Rockport, Mass., 1938,
7-11/16 × 9-5/8" (19.6 × 24.4 cm)
Boy Climbing Wall, Rockport, Mass.,
1938, 7½ × 9½" (19 × 24.2 cm)
Shipwreck, Rockport, Mass., 1938
7½ × 9½" (19 × 24.2 cm)
Wooden Figure, Atlantic City, 1938
7-3/8 × 9½" (18.7 × 24.2 cm)
Sara Mazo, 1938
7 × 9½" (17.7 × 24.2 cm)
Karl Fortess, 1938
9-5/16 × 7½" (17.7 × 24.2 cm)
Coney Island; Boardwalk and Bather,
1938, 7¾" × 9½"
Children, Coney Island, 1938
7½ × 9½" (19 × 24.25 cm)
Private collection, Florida
Black Man on Beach, 1938
7-3/8 × 9-3/8" (18.8 × 24 cm)
Boy Floating, Rockport, Mass., 1938
7-9/16 × 9-5/8" (19.2 × 24.5 cm)
Boys Diving off Pier, 1938
7-5/8 × 9½" (19.4 × 24.1 cm)
Boys Wrestling, 1938
7-9/16 × 9½" (19.2 × 24.2 cm)
Sara and Glass Table-Top, 1938
9-9/16 × 7-5/8" (24.3 × 19.4 cm)
Andree Ruellan and Elsie Speicher,
1938, 7-9/16 × 9-9/16"
(19.2 × 24.3 cm)
Sara and Inez, 1938
9-7/16 × 7-9/16" (24 × 19.2 cm)
Nude, 1938
8 × 10" (20.3 × 25.3 cm)
Fish Market, 1938
7-9/16 × 9-7/16" (19.2 × 23.9 cm)
East Kingston, 1938
7-5/8 × 9-7/16" (19.4 × 23.9 cm)
Union Square, 1938
7-1/8 × 9-5/8" (18.1 × 24.5 cm)
Union Square in Snow, 1938
9-3/8 × 7-9/16" (23.9 × 19.2 cm)
Collection Norton Gallery and
School of Art
Union Square in Snow, 1938
8 × 10" (20.3 × 25.3 cm)
Ceiling, Glass Building, World's Fair,
1939, 7½ × 9-5/16"
(19 × 23.3 cm)
Arch, World's Fair, 1939
7-7/15 × 9-5/8" (18.9 × 24.4 cm)
Mother and Child, The South, 1939
9-5/8 × 7½" (24.4 × 19 cm)
Black Child, The South, 1939
7-9/16 × 9-7/16" (19.3 × 23.0 cm)
World's Fair Ceiling, 1939
9-5/8 × 7-9/16" (24.5 × 19.2 cm)
Fun House Mirror, 1939
7-7/16 × 9½" (18.9 × 24.2 cm)
Negro Couples, 1939
7-9/16 × 9-9/16" (19.2 × 24.3 cm)
Shadows, n.d.
7-5/16 × 9-5/16" (18.5 × 23.3 cm)
Woman in Crowd, n.d.
7-3/16 × 9-7/16" (18.3 × 24.3 cm)

Mrs. H. Knight, n.d.
9½ × 7-7/16" (24.2 × 18.9 cm)
Reginald Marsh, n.d.
7-1/8 × 9½" (18 × 24.2 cm)
Snow, Philadelphia, n.d.
7-9/16 × 9-9/16" (19.3 × 24.3 cm)
*Sara Kuniyoshi, Jean and Julian
Levy*, n.d., 7¼ × 9-9/16"
(18.3 × 24.3 cm)
St. John's Daughters, n.d.
7½ × 9-9/16" (19.1 × 24.3 cm)
Carousel Horse, n.d.
7-9/16 × 9-9/16" (19.2 × 24.3 cm)
Collection Mr. and Mrs. Jim Sullivan,
New York

PAINTINGS

Weathervane and Other Objects, 1933
Oil on canvas, 35¼ × 60-1/8"
Collection of the Santa Barbara Museum
of Art, Gift of Wright Ludington
Things on an Iron Chair, 1936
Oil on canvas, 44¼ × 34"
Collection of the Whitney Museum of
American Art. Given in memory of
Edith Gregor Halpert by the Halpert
Foundation, 1975
I Think So, 1938
Oil on canvas, 40 × 31"
Collection of the Albright-Knox
Art Gallery, Room of Contemporary
Art Fund, 1939
Deserted Brickyard, 1938
Oil on canvas, 20-1/8 × 35¼"
Collection of the Honolulu Academy of
Arts. Gift of Philip E. Spalding, 1949
Lay Figure, 1938
Oil on canvas, 38-1/8 × 58¼
Collection of the Walker Art Center,
Minneapolis. Gift of
The T. B. Walker Foundation
Accordion, 1938
Oil on canvas, 38-1/8 × 48"
Lent by the Metropolitan Museum of Art.
The Edward Joseph Gallagher III
Memorial Collection. Gift of Edward J.
Gallagher, Jr., 1955
Standing Nude, 1939-41
Maroger, 16 × 12"
Collection of Paul Jenkins
Upside Down Table and Mask, 1940
Oil on canvas, 60-1/8 × 35½"
Collection of the Museum of Modern
Art, NY. Acquired through the
Lilie P. Bliss Bequest, 1944
My Man, c. 1943
Casein on board, 14-3/4 × 10½"
Collection of The Art Institute of
Chicago. Olivia Shaler Swan Memorial
Room 110, 1944
Oil on canvas, 44 × 34"
F. M. Hall Collection, Sheldon Memorial
Art Gallery, University of
Nebraska-Lincoln

Broken Objects, 1944
Oil on canvas, 30 × 50¼"
Lent by the Metropolitan Museum of Art.
Gift of Mr. and Mrs. Allan D. Emil, 1963
Rotting on the Shore, 1945
Oil on canvas, 46-1/8 × 36-1/8"
Collection of the Norton Gallery and
School of Art

LITHOGRAPHS

Pears, Grapes, and Peaches, 1927
Transfer lithograph, 16 × 12-5/8"
(40.7 × 32.1 cm) Collection of the
Museum of Modern Art. Gift of Abby
Aldrich Rockefeller
Pipe and Cigars, 1932
Lithograph, 9-1/8 × 14-7/16"
(23.2 × 36.7 cm) Collection
of the Museum of Modern Art.
Given anonymously
Artificial Flower, 1934
Lithograph, 16¼ × 10¼"
(41.3 × 26 cm)
Collection of the Museum of
Modern Art. Given anonymously
Trapeze Girl, 1936
Lithograph, 13 × 10"
(32.9 × 25.5 cm)
Collection of the Museum of Modern
Art. Given anonymously
From the Boardwalk, 1936
Lithograph, 9¼ × 12-5/16"
(23.5 × 31.3 cm) Collection
of the Museum of Modern Art.
Given anonymously

DRAWINGS

The Swimmer, 1924
Ink on paper, 14-3/4 × 17-7/8"
Collection of the Whitney Museum of
American Art. Gift of Mr. and Mrs.
Charles J. Liebman, 1948
Abandoned Building, c. 1930
Pencil on paper, 11 × 17"
Private collection
Girl Reading, c. 1930
Pencil on paper, 17 × 14"
Private collection
Deserted Brickyard (study), 1938
Pencil on paper, 11 × 17"
Private collection

*All photographs were borrowed from
the collection of Sara Kuniyoshi unless
otherwise noted.*

YASUO KUNIYOSHI:
ARTIST AS PHOTOGRAPHER

Fig. 1. Yasuo Kuniyoshi, Mexico, 1935, photograph, 10-11/16 × 9½"

(All photographs were borrowed from the collection of Sara Kuniyoshi unless otherwise noted.)

Fig. 2. Yasuo Kuniyoshi, From the Boardwalk, 1936, photograph, 7-3/8 × 9-3/8"

Fig. 3. Yasuo Kuniyoshi, Coney Island; Boardwalk and Bathers, *1938, photograph, 7½ × 9½"*

Fig. 4. Yasuo Kuniyoshi, Children, Coney Island, 1938, photograph, 7¾ × 9½"
Private Collection, Florida

Fig. 5. *Yasuo Kuniyoshi, Boys Diving off Pier*, 1938, photograph, 7-5/8 × 9½"

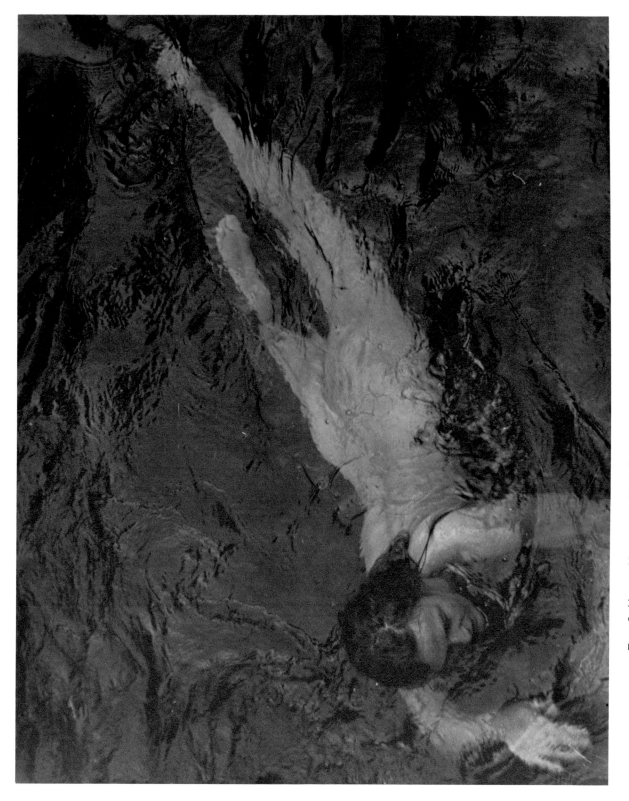

Fig. 6. Yasuo Kuniyoshi, Rosella Hartman Swimming, 1937, photograph, 8 × 10"

Fig. 7. Yasuo Kuniyoshi, Boy Floating, Rockport Mass., 1938, photograph, 7½ × 9-5/8"

Fig. 8. Yasuo Kuniyoshi, Boys Wrestling, 1938, photograph, 7½ × 9½"

Fig. 9. Yasuo Kuniyoshi, World's Fair Ceiling, 1939, photograph, 9.5/8 × 7½"

Fig. 10. Yasuo Kuniyoshi, Sara and Glass Table-Top, *1938, photograph, 9½ × 7-5/8"*

Fig. 11. Yasuo Kuniyoshi, Sara and Inez, *1938, photograph, 9½ × 7½"*

Fig. 12. Yasuo Kuniyoshi, Andrée Ruellan and Elsie Speicher, 1938, photograph, 7½ × 9½"

Fig. 13. Yasuo Kuniyoshi, St. John's Daughters, nd., photograph, 7½ × 9½"

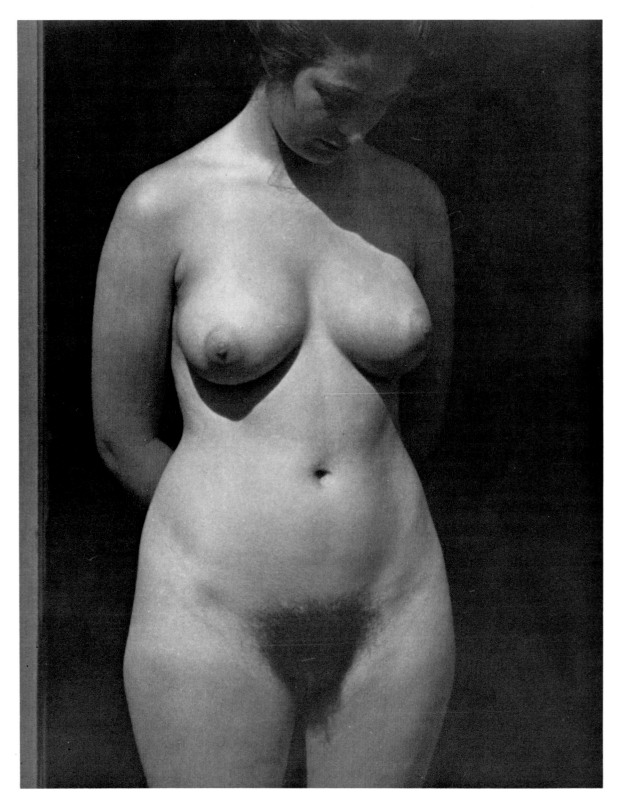

Fig. 14. Yasuo Kuniyoshi, Model, *1937, photograph, 9½ × 7½"*

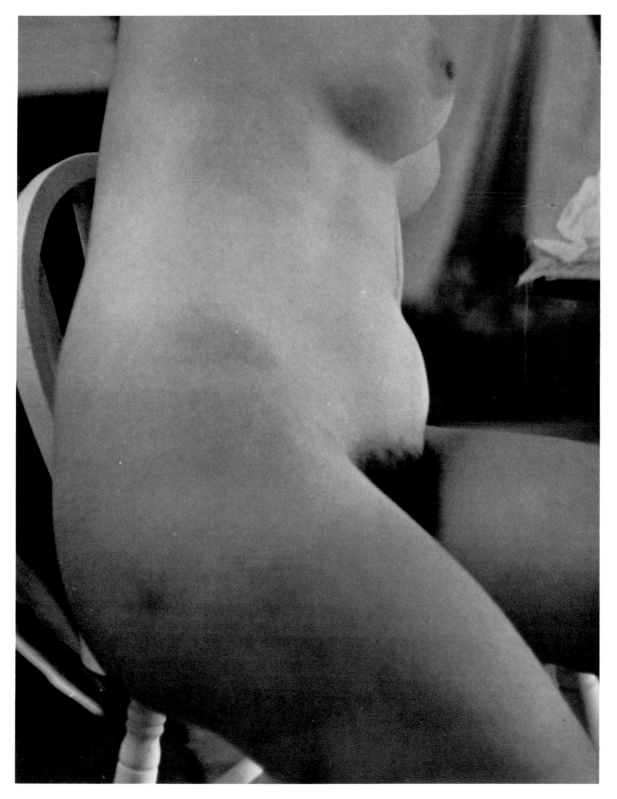

Fig. 15. Yasuo Kuniyoshi, Torso, *1937, photograph, 9½ × 7½"*

Fig. 16. Yasuo Kuniyoshi, Nude, *1936, photograph, 8 × 10"*

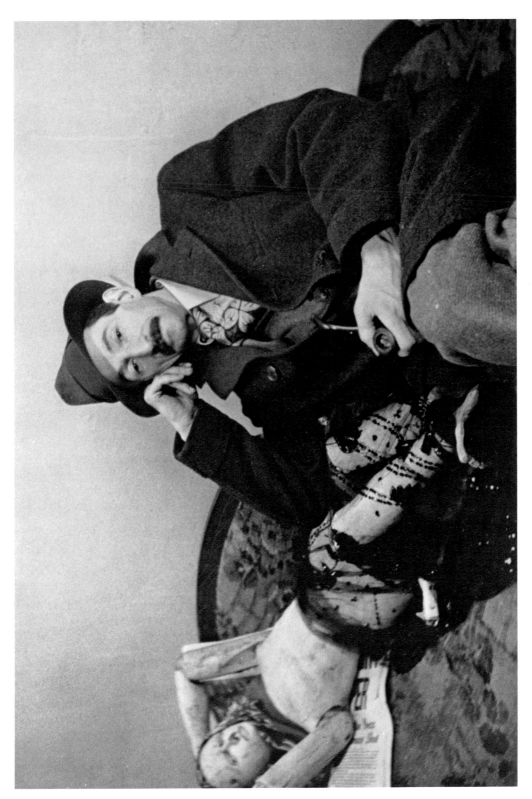

Fig. 17. Yasuo Kuniyoshi, Morris Kantor, 1938, photograph, 6-3/8 × 9¼"

Fig. 18. Yasuo Kuniyoshi, Carousel Horse, nd., photograph, 7½ × 9½"
Collection of Mr. and Mrs. Jim Sullivan, New York

Fig. 19. *Yasuo Kuniyoshi, Fun House Mirror, 1939, photograph, 7½ × 9½"*

Fig. 20. Yasuo Kuniyoshi, May Day Parade, 1937, photograph, 7½ × 9½"

Fig. 21. Yasuo Kuniyoshi, Fish Market, 1938, photograph, 7½ × 9½"

Fig. 22. Yasuo Kuniyoshi, Negro Couples, 1939, photograph, 7½ × 9½"

Fig. 23. Yasuo Kuniyoshi, East Kingston, 1938, photograph, 7-5/8 × 9½"

Fig. 24. Yasuo Kuniyoshi, Abandoned Woodshed, 1937, photograph, 7¼ × 9½"

Fig. 25. Yasuo Kuniyoshi, Abandoned Woodshed, Texture, 1937, photograph, 7¼ × 9½"

Fig. 26. Yasuo Kuniyoshi, Union Square, 1938, photograph, 7-1/8 × 9-5/8"

Fig. 27. Yasuo Kuniyoshi, Union Square in Snow, photograph, 8 × 10"
Collection of the Norton Gallery and School of Art

Fig. 28. Yasuo Kuniyoshi, Union Square in Snow, *1938, photograph, 9-3/8 × 7½"*

PAINTER-PHOTOGRAPHERS
The 1930s, the 35mm Camera

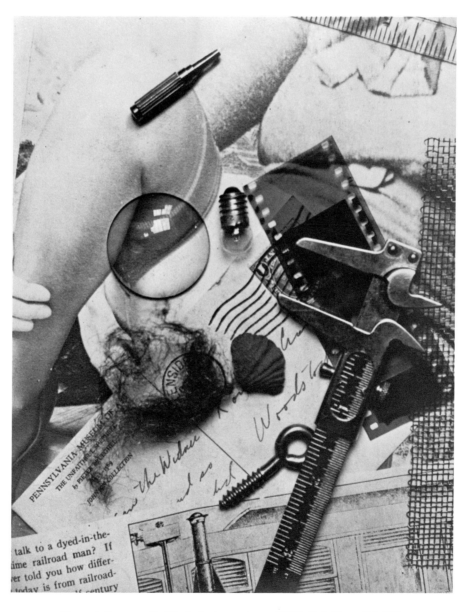

Konrad Cramer, Untitled photograph, c. 1930, 9-1/2 × 7-1/2"
Courtesy Photofind Gallery, Woodstock, NY

Rockwell Kent, "Greenland—Jakobs Harn"
Photograph, c. 1930 4-7/8 × 7". Collection Rockwell Kent Legacies

Ralston Crawford, "Jean Beckwith (Mrs Chester Miller)", 1940-41, 5 3/3 × 8"
Collection Ralston Crawford Estate. Courtesy Robert Miller Gallery, New York

Reginald Marsh, Untitled photograph, c. 1930, 6 × 9-1/2"
Museum of the City of New York. Bequest of Felicia Meyer Marsh

Ben Shahn, Untitled photograph, c. 1930, 6 × 9-1/2"
Collection Bermanda Bryson Shahn